MW00893475

The New Now
Manifestos, Reinventions & Declarations
Updated & Expanded

Copyrighted © 2023
Russell C. Smith & Michael Foster.

All rights reserved.

No part of this book may be reproduced, or stored in a retrieval system, or transmitted in any form or by any means, electronic, mechanical, photocopying, recording, or otherwise, without express written permission of the publisher.

2nd Edition - 1st Printing

Cover design by: Michael Foster

Printed by Amazon

The New Now

Manifestos, Reinventions & Declarations
Updated & Expanded

Russell C. Smith
& Michael Foster

Dedications:

Russell C. Smith
Dedicated to Tricia King

Michael Foster
For J

Contents

Manifestos, Reinventions & Declarations / Updated & Expanded

The New Now / Manifestos, Reinventions & Declarations / Updated & Expanded is a book about the New Now we're living in and going through.

After experiencing a global pandemic rolling across and ravaging our land, we can more easily understand how historic and prehistoric events actually happened. Now, with deeply embedded wrongheaded cultural norms being pushed against as never before, we can also understand how societal shifts sometimes happened in past centuries, within months, days, or hours, and when a tipping point was finally reached.

We all experienced how the whole planet put on pause was a major worldwide event. Since so much has changed within a few years' time, we felt that the historic times we were in had transformed our culture and our world enough to add to the book we published in the summer of 2020.

• Times have drastically changed in a few years' time. Authoritarians have taken over or are trying to take over, everywhere in the world.

• One way that authoritarians and fascists try to control people is by restricting information, in the form of books, news, movies, music, podcasts, blogs, videos, and the Internet itself. The un-democratic and un-American book banning going on across America is a part of this global thought police sickness.

• What was a Cold Civil War has heated up, and we've become the Divided States of America. When Democracy itself is on the ballot, we're living through strange times. When reality itself needs protecting, we've gone through the looking glass.

• We've revisited the topic of lowering the voting age, this time to 16-years-old, which would let our youngest politically-involved citizens have the right to vote on the issues most directly impacting their lives—gun control laws, the Climate Emergency, and censorship in the form of book banning.

Collectively, in the back of our minds, a part of us knew a massive shift could or would eventually happen. We've all been dreaming of, or expecting some type of change to happen. Although we weren't expecting anything as drastic and cultural/world shifting as what happened.

We all want to change our own lives for the better, and now it truly feels like it should also include the lives of others. Without time to plan for this, it felt like it happened in an instant.

So, if anyone needed any proof, yes, we are definitely all one.

If we believe we possess the power to change ourselves, then the same has to be true for positively shifting the culture. Transforming our culture into a more empathetic, generous, and tolerant culture is worth the effort. And this is the ideal historic moment to do so. If not now, when?

For the updated & expanded version of our book, we've added these eight new pieces: The End of

Authoritarianism, Living in the New Now (There's Never Going to Be a New Normal), Looking for the Good, A Manifesto on Manifestos, America has a book banning problem, From Seattle to Brooklyn, Public libraries have stood up against book banning, Living in the Divided States of America (It's now unmistakable. We're living in two separate countries.), and A Declaration of Interdependence #4. Along with the gun violence epidemic, and the Climate Crisis ramping up, we highlight what's being done to push back against banning, burning, and censorship in this revised and updated version of our book. Fast forward, several years past 2020, and our world is in more turmoil with more at stake as far as building the future we want to live in, and we have a clarity that probably wasn't possible even a mere two years ago. History is being made at an accelerated pace, and we're all in a new world, often shifting daily and weekly.

How we act, speak up, vote, communicate locally and globally matters more than ever before.

Clear choices are on the table. Freedom vs. Authoritarianism. Democracy vs. Theocracy. Freedom of Thought vs. Book Banning. Women's Healthcare and Reproductive Rights vs. Taking Away Hard-Won Victories.

With these eight new and updated manifestos and essays, both subject matter and tone reflect the gravity of where we are in the New Now, and just how much the world has shifted under our feet in such a short amount of time.

In the 2023 edition of The New Now / Manifestos, Reinventions & Declarations, we now dig into these topics in a more direct way.

• The Climate Crisis has worsened and sped up, and it's clear we've reached the tipping point that was predicted, quite clearly in Al Gore's 2006 documentary, An Inconvenient Truth. In 2022, Superstorms were upgraded to Storms of the Century, and rainfall totals of a decade's worth of rain happened over a four-day nonstop deluge. After superstorm hurricane Ian pummeled Cuba, it smashed into Florida's Gulf Coast midsection, flooding and destroying whole cities and communities. Climate Emergency deniers continued not to believe their own eyes as a superstorm of this magnitude engulfed an entire state. How is it even possible to hate/fear/deny reality that much?

• An authoritarian, murderous dictator invaded Ukraine and committed mass genocide and torture, targeting civilians and children. The horrors have been documented; the brutal genocide has continued by a terrorist state. They've threatened the world with nuclear warfare—while a pandemic still raged in the background.

- In Iran, a 22-year-old woman was murdered by the (morality?) police for not covering up her head with a piece of cloth in the exact way an extremist authoritarian theocratic regime tells her she should. Brutalized and murdered for a piece of cloth? Nothing remotely moral about that. Murdering protesters by public hanging has nothing to do with morality. It has to do with a murderous theocratic government that's lost its grip on several generations of its citizens. When no one believes you anymore, your theocracy has reached a dead end.

- Gun violence, in the form of weekly mass shootings with easily purchased AR-15 rifles. These weapons of war have become so devastatingly destructive in the United States that many of us are one person removed from knowing someone who has moved to Europe to escape the ongoing epidemic of gun violence.

- It's time to expand voting rights and lower the voting age, using technology so more people will participate in democracy, especially for the youth of America. Taking the current Climate Crisis and the future of the world into account, we believe the voting age should be lowered to 16 years old. Our voting system should be a countrywide vote by mail, and as soon as possible a vote online system. Then we'll see a youth voter turnout! Smartphone voting anyone?

• Healthcare and reproductive rights were taken away by an extremist far-right Supreme Court, stripping women of a fundamental (which the newly appointed supreme court justices agreed they wouldn't do, in their televised job interviews woman's healthcare right that had been a legal precedent since 1973. Women's right to autonomy over their own reproductive rights must be expanded and protected, so they can't be taken away by judicial extremism. To that point, the Respect for Marriage Act is passed by Congress, in December 2022, protecting same-sex and interracial marriages, preemptively putting up a barrier around loving hearts and blocking further judicial extremism. Love is love, has been codified into federal law and one political party can't prevent two human beings from loving each other as they see fit. A strong message was sent to the authoritarians of the United States.

- When book banning and book burning steps out of the pages of a dystopian science fiction novel and rears its extremist fascist face in states like Florida and Texas, the future of Freedom of Thought/ Freethinking is on the line. And this is exactly where we have to draw the line—if the words freedom and democracy still possess any meaning.

- Authoritarianism, in the form of a violent insurrection, nearly overthrew the United States government on January 6, 2021, and one political party took it seriously and the other shrugged it off. Democracy itself is at a crossroads. On Dec 19, 2022, The January 6 Committee made four criminal referrals to the Justice Department, recommending the former President be investigated. At the top of the list is inciting, assisting, or aiding and comforting an insurrection. In late February 2022 at the start of the War in Ukraine, President Zelensky stood up for his country and made the historic statement: "The fight is here; I need ammunition, not a ride." On December 21, 2022, President Zelensky flew into the United States, met with President Biden, and delivered a historic speech to a joint meeting of Congress. In the speech he thanked every American for helping Ukraine defend itself against the brutal terrorist invasion committed by Russia. In the early morning hours of January 7,

2023, after the longest battle for House Speaker since the Civil War, Republicans begrudgingly let their guy get in, and speaker Hakeem Jeffries praised Speaker Nancy Pelosi, by saying "She will go down in history as the greatest speaker of all time. Calling her a "legendary legislator, a fabulous facilitator and a no-nonsense negotiator." Then, Hakeem Jeffries (D-NY), the first Black man elected to be Minority Leader of the House, gave a preview of how Democrats will govern during these historically divided times in the Divided States of America. Here's a section of it: "I also want to make clear that we will never compromise our principles. House Democrats will always put: American values over autocracy. Benevolence over bigotry. The Constitution over the cult. Democracy over demagogues. Economic opportunity over extremism. Freedom over fascism. Governing over gaslighting. Hopefulness over hatred. Inclusion over isolation. Justice over judicial overreach. Knowledge over kangaroo courts. Liberty over limitation. Maturity over Mar-a-Lago. Normalcy over negativity. Opportunity over obstruction." Brilliant. Brilliant. Brilliant. In America, while the Cold Civil War heats up on the front burner of daily life, we keep looking for Life, Liberty, and the Pursuit of Happiness. Many of us are always on the lookout for the Truth. And sometimes it shines through in the unlikeliest of places, like the floor of Congress. We must remember that Election Deniers don't believe in a peaceful transition of power. Many of the far-right extremist Election Deniers were elected to Congress, so staying vigilant against the authoritarian mindset is an essential fact of living through these times. Authoritarianism and those who prefer it over Democracy are on the wrong side of history.

One of the themes we put into the first version of this book is the idea of The New Now, since it clearly describes what had just happened to humanity, on a global scale. Countless pundits, newscasters, heads of corporations, and politicians were quick to call an end to the pandemic, and stress that we're living with a New Normal. So much so that the phrase became annoying quite quickly.

Dear Everyone, there's never going to be a New Normal, and who'd even wish for such a thing. It's not going to happen. There is no New Normal to go back to, or move toward. There's nothing normal about accepting "that's the way we've always done it" since so many actions, behaviors, and modes of being that were casually accepted just weren't good for millions of people, and certainly not for everyone. Goodbye forever "New Normal" and don't let the screen door hit you in the ass on the way out. You're not welcome here in the New Now.

We see this nearly post-pandemic world (keep your masks handy) as a new start, after an honest to goodness cultural and social reset. It felt like, wow, it's really happening. An event on par with an alien invasion. Every post-apocalyptic sci-fi movie we've watched over the course of our lives, was disrupting all human life on the planet, in real-time and on a visceral level. Why would a "New Normal" that's just a glossed-over longing for the same old normal so many had been trying every day to escape from, be even remotely acceptable? Clearly, the power-grabbing, murderous, authoritarian dictators in every corner of the world don't feel this way. They are in love with what they could get away with in the old normal, and wanted a New Normal that meant more of the same for them. They decided to wage war and commit genocide while the world was doing its best to survive. The constant senseless killing isn't normal.

The rest of humanity that wants to live caring, peaceful, creative, and fun lives, went in the other direction. We're living in the New Now. Doing our best to continue to alter society by helping to bring about more tolerance, diversity, compassion, intelligence, free-thinking—and everything that goes with it, including supporting commonsense politicians who truly believe their own senses and understand that the Climate Crisis is real.

How we act, speak up, vote, communicate locally and globally matters more than ever before. Clear choices are on the table. Freedom vs. Authoritarianism. Democracy vs. Theocracy. Freedom of Thought vs. Book Banning. Women's Healthcare and Reproductive Rights vs. Taking Away Hard-Won Victories. With these eight new and updated manifestos and essays, both subject matter and tone reflect the gravity of where we are in the New Now, and just how much the world has shifted under our feet in such a short amount of time.

Living in the New Now

There's never going to be a New Normal

The New Now is right in front of our faces. The personal is universal, and the universal is personal. The time is now. We are all one human family.

Recent news in the New Now: A murderous tyrant invades and attempts to steal a country before dawn's early light. He sent badly trained murderous soldiers across the border and David stood up to Goliath. Whapped the tyrant in the eye with a rock the size of a boulder. Clocks in the town square began running backwards. More senseless mass shootings than you can count happened, every single week—

elementary school kids were murdered by weapons of war—we stood up, said hell no, enough is enough! Something was finally done about it. Sadly, not enough. Big money spoke, and taking these weapons of war away from easy reach didn't happen. Once again. Mass shootings in the hate crime category by domestic terrorists are still the order of the day. The mob violently stormed the Capitol, killing and wounding as the day of insurrection went on. Many were held accountable. Many were not. Before the midterms, a tweet was tweeted, then deleted, then retweeted in another context. The cold civil war has been placed on the front burner. Murdering drag queens and targeting the electrical grid is now part of the war. The blue wall held back a red mirage that was supposed to be a wave. Women's fundamental healthcare rights were stolen in the dark of night by a tainted Supreme Court, and women marched and shouted from coast to coast. Saying no, no more, not this time. They stood up for the hard-won rights that were stolen away from them. They shouted, "We've come too far to let history go backwards. We're not going to pass along a world that doesn't include control of our bodies on to the next generation." In the halls of Congress, far-right extremists fiddle around, preening for their social media moment while the planet burns.

Humanity is streaming across the border, through the cracks made in history.

History's Hinge has swung wide open and opened us up. We've gone through a series of reboots over the past several years—Covid-19, a violent insurrection against the U.S. Government, the brutal and senseless invasion of Ukraine, the climate crisis ratcheting up a few degrees, malevolent authoritarian dictators who go so far as to threaten nuclear war, the global collapse of eco-systems—one can get the feeling the world's trying to tell humanity something.

Change direction now? Change hearts and minds? Change the global narrative? Stop using fossil fuels? Survival of the human species, anyone?

Where is love, common sense, caring for each other and the world?

We're living in a New Now. Living through history in the making. Watching a war half a world away with someone's mobile phone always set on record.

Don't believe the world must keep repeating the same lies, reinforcing the actions of the same terrible tyrants or corrupt politicians, accept the same horrific actions leading to countless senseless deaths.

You don't have to believe any of these lies for one more second. It's not serving life, democracy, freedom, or reality to keep believing falsehoods made of ignorance and wasted breath.

We're not living in the kind of world where we have to agree with gaslighting, spewed by delusionary minds.

If you woke up today, in the New Now, you've proven to yourself how the world changes. Today isn't yesterday. This Now isn't yesterday's Now. Now is the moment to live in a free world, in your own reality, following your own path, breaking from the lies of the past, and saying no to murderous control systems and yes to thinking your own thoughts.

Say no to the wrongheaded ones who want to keep the clocks running backwards. Say yes to the people with open hearts and minds.

The New Now has learned a few important lessons. The world finally understands this—all bullies are cowards at heart. Let's put iron in our spines and stand up to fake lying leaders. Who needs them? Enough is enough! Bullies don't control lives in the New Now. They are fading from history, becoming invisible as you read these words.

Change the path history's on by standing up. Change how you experience the world. See it with new eyes. Reject all propaganda and lies, which never should've been normalized.

In the New Now, we're living inside every moment—everywhen and everynow.

We are creating the history of these times.

The world was on pause, and it's up and running again. (Even though the pandemic is still going on.) Let's be clear. There's never going to be a New Normal. It's not even a thing to wish for. Stop saying it or even thinking it. Tell your local media stations to stop asking when we'll be getting back to Normal. Never going to be such a thing, ever again.

The previous Normal left out too many human beings, who wanted to be let in. It's the end of senseless social norms we were told to accept. Finally, the dust fell from our eyes, and with new-found clarity we saw through the big lies written in the sky.

The previous faulty Normal didn't include teaching emotional intelligence and meditation to children, peace and prosperity as a basic human right, healthcare coverage for all, an end to the never-ending reign of dictators and tyrants the world over, putting an end to the American gun violence epidemic, saying yes to love and abundance for everyone, and saying no to ongoing senseless cycles of war.

Let's create a reality where world peace is possible. How about it?

It's time to change laws, rules of governance, how many years supreme court justices can serve, and how much money politicians can take (in the form of legal bribery) from organizations and corporations.

It's time to say yes to the future of our planet and say no to corporations run only with greed as the primary motivating factor.

It's time to live in a land where when social change happens after decades of struggle, those changes can't be reversed.

It's time to promote and believe in the arts of the New Now. Books (start with reading books from a list of the most often banned books), paintings, poetry (we're living in a new golden age of poetry), movement, music, multi-sensory art forms, photography, visionary dream-like movies and videos. Whatever you can imagine and create. Art forms are here to open up minds. It's up to you. Always has been.

The New Now isn't living in a sci-fi metaverse, it's already in our hearts.

In the New Now, books and free thought aren't banned by backwards-thinking humans in states where clocks are running backwards. If you're afraid of books and thinking, and young people having open-minded thoughts, you must be in a constant state of inner terror, turmoil, and fear. Try taking a walk to relieve your stress. It's recommended on the Internet.

In the New Now, education is a wide-open universe of unending knowledge. Taking in knowledge from books you choose to pick up and read is as essential as breathing. It's an act of personal freedom. You can never learn too much, or read too many diverse and thought provoking and wondrous books. Reading a writer is entering the mind and world of another human being. There are more and more books being published every year. Banning books could literally drive one mad from over-thinking which wonderful new imaginative caring thoughts you can't stand.

Why do humans think they can possibly prevent others from becoming smarter through the power of reading? Add to that, an endless degree of trying to tamp down the mental growth of the youth, middle-aged, and seniors of our country. By attempting to prevent other humans from forming their own thoughts by reading books of their own choosing, you've spent a lot of energy on nothing you could've ever prevented in a million years. Why would anyone on Earth want to spend their time in such a fruitless pursuit? The war against ideas is never going to be won by the closed-minded. The power of the written word will prevail. Books open minds to new ideas, which is how humanity has always moved forward—with open, imaginative minds.

In the New Now, human rights and personal rights are one, and they can't be stolen by corrupt politicians, or by pitting one color-coded state against another. Let's all admit racism has always been wrongheaded, horrific, ignorant, and it's long past time to change minds and hearts for good. Hate has only served to keep hearts blindly hating other humans based upon skin color, sexual orientation, religious misinterpretations, social customs, and a whole list of other socially backwards factors—meant only to divide cultures and start wars.

The New Now wants you to start by looking inside, and making friends with your own tender heart. Be open to new ideas. Become larger in spirit and in curiosity. Practice generosity. Shift our culture forward into the future. Help to create a place where our expansive nature has a place to breathe freely, and we'll become generous, peaceful, empathetic human beings.

The End of Authoritarianism

We're at a turning point in history.

We've reached a Hinge of History. Can you feel it?
Like a strong wind, can you feel a global shift in
everything that was before?

Put your hand over your heart and feel your breath
moving in and out.

We are in a New Now. The choice is either a world of
war or peace. And it's decision time.

You think you've heard this before. But wait,
there's more.

Now, in 2023, the era of dictatorships, autocracies, theocracies, and totalitarian regimes is over.

Authoritarians, history has stuck a pin in your story, and put you in the history books as a done deal. You were a part of a failed global cultural structure, meant only to destructively harm people in your country, and the countries you invaded. So, build a time machine and head back to the Dark Ages where you'll feel more at home.

In the year 2023, the authoritarian mindset has reached a dead end.

Authoritarianism is a cancer on every society and culture, where it has taken hold and destroyed lives.

It's either one way or the other—and the stakes are high. One is choosing life, love, peace, and living joyfully—and the other is accepting pointless death at the hand of psychopaths. Human beings no longer want to be murdered for the sake of one controlling dictator's mentally unhinged, faulty historical, or dangerous religious notions. Every reason that's given on TV news about why someone decided to kill a person or a people, is a meaningless reason. It's time for a global ceasefire. Stop the killing now!

Globally, authoritarianism must be brought to an end, wherever it has infiltrated and sought to destroy a society from within—by means of daily doses of poison lies, incessant propaganda, or nightly fabricated falsehoods and misdirection pretending to be news—it has poisoned the culture.

Humans everywhere on this planet have stood up, and history has made it clear. Their eyes have been opened, and they aren't willing to close them again. No, not anymore! It's over! The vile and horrific perpetrators of brutal wars, and destructive theocratic control systems must be held accountable. No more senseless murderous thuggery, and genocidal killing. While these words are being written, torture and genocide is happening. Human beings are being slaughtered by an invading army for meaningless lies. Russia's invasion of Ukraine is a horrific stain on the legacy of every Russian leader and anyone who's in Russia's military for generations to come.

In the United States, our own slaughter of the innocents happens on a weekly basis. When those profiting from the sale of military grade weapons let us know they are on the side of more deaths, let's believe them. Automatic weapons are being bought as easily as going down to the corner convenience store and buying a soda. For decades, children have been buying weapons of war to kill other children. Death profiteers must be held accountable. Politicians who don't care about freedom, liberty, free thinking— must be voted out of office.

Death happens in an instant, so must the response to mass murder—whether in a democratic country invaded by an unhinged madman, or in an elementary school classroom in the land of the free and the home of the brave.

War is terrorism, when brought to you by a despicable maniac, who at heart is a cowardly bully. A bully is just a coward wearing a see-through mask.

War is happening as lawless murdering thugs, killing, raping, looting. Which isn't war, it's terrorism. Murder committed by pretend soldiers thinking they are free from international laws against war crimes.

War as the killing of countless civilians—from newborns to those who want to live out their last days and hours in peace.

Make war an unprofitable business. Make selling authoritarian violence and weapons of war to the misinformed, misled, and lovers of violence among us a broken business model.

Enough is enough! It can go no further, after the most horrifically violent dictatorial regime since Hitler's has committed brutal atrocities the whole world is aware of—killing babies and pregnant mothers, raping women, senselessly murdering old people who had nowhere else to go.

Brutal soldiers carried out the orders from on high, and then failed in a cover-up by partially burning bodies. When all this wasn't enough horror to be heaped upon the people of Ukraine, they added landmines to blow apart schools and homes as they ran away from their war crimes. These were no soldiers, these were violent cowards killing innocent people for zero reasons.

This is 2023, not 1943. We carry around the Internet in our pockets. Russia's unconscionable invasion is viewed in an instant, in the immediate moment the horrific murders happen. The brutality of how dictatorships are run has been made visceral, palpable, and personal to everyone everywhere.

All the destruction and mass murders are happening with a backdrop of the existential threat of an ongoing Climate Crisis. Our world is in crisis and World War III is happening. The leveling of cities. Mass graves. Erasing a country's culture. All in a matter of months. Mass genocide has been transmitted to the communication device you carry in your pocket.

Any authoritarian dictator who thinks the world will put up with this insanity during the time of a global pandemic, while a climate crisis is threatening all life on planet Earth is living in their own delusional chamber of horrors. Killing innocents won't fill the void in their black hearts.

Enough is enough! America was sold countless lies about why stricter gun laws couldn't, wouldn't, shouldn't happen. And here we are, decades after Columbine, asked to witness and somehow understand one more horrific killing spree by a young man who shouldn't have been able to purchase an AR-15 assault rifle. One more person who thought the answer to his problems was to buy military-grade rifles and kill innocent school children. What we see is money = murder. Murder of innocent lives. For far too long.

We live in a world of such love and such violence. Such beauty and such tragedy. Ongoing wars usually based on pure authoritarian stupidity and murderous hearts.

At the very least, the mantra for all of it must be "Enough is Enough!" Now that we should be long past the time of lies and gaslighting, can those who are behind the horrific violence stand up and speak up, at long last, and even whisper the words: "Enough is Enough!" along with everyone else?

A 22-year-old woman in Iran, named Mahsa Amini, was killed by a brutal arm of their totalitarian theocratic regime. She was brutally murdered for just living her life, by the so-called morality police. Do they hate women to the core of their beings? Rioting in the streets every night since after she was brutally murdered tells the world "Enough is Enough!"

We can feel the future looking back at us, wondering why it took so long to act upon the Climate Crisis, the insanity of authoritarian control systems, enforcing theocratic rules and laws that shouldn't even exist in this century, the gun violence epidemic, the descent of a culture into willful stupidity. Will they shake their heads in wonder, or just be disgusted? Will our future global citizens be thinking "We would have seen through the never-ending barrage of toxic lies; we would've found a way to change the whole system sooner."

Authoritarianism is in the process of destroying the foundation of a free-thinking, democratic culture, from the inside-out. Authoritarianism must be brought to a quick end. It's best for the culture, and for all humanity on planet Earth. If we go, it all goes. Generation after generation came here for the ideal of freedom, and for decades now it's been thrown back in their faces, eroded around them, made a mockery of their ancestors and what they built with a belief that nothing could stop the future from getting brighter and brighter, for all those in their lineage who came after them.

Authoritarianism is against personal freedom, women, love, kindness, open minds, people who think for themselves, social justice, reading books, the environment, new ideas, asking questions, creating a society where we are all cared for.

Do you believe Democracy's time has come and gone? Are you OK with letting it go with a shrug? Or are we as a culture, ready to help wake everyone up from the stupor? We can see it just ahead, past the next dead end road sign—the total end of authoritarianism.

We're living on a Hinge of History. The time is right now. We're going to get rid of dictators, the autocratic mindset, and theocratic authoritarians—and create a more livable planet, culture, and way of being. We no longer have a choice. Authoritarians have brought about their own end. Forget them. They are in history's review mirror. They no longer matter. Remember how good feeling alive feels. Remember that people vote and march and change the world. Right now, let's declare the end of authoritarianism. It's gone too far, taken away too much, and destroyed too many lives. Stand up and speak up. What else can we do?

Looking for the Good

Looking around, it's easy to see the current state of America in 2023 as a dumpster fire at the end of a dark alley on a wintry night. The Cold Civil War has turned hot. People are fleeing the country to escape the gun violence epidemic. The Climate Crisis has turned into a dystopian science-fiction film, and The Handmaid's Tale has become a documentary.

Will any deeper answers surface about the January 6, 2021, insurrection, and serve to hold those accountable at the top of the political food chain? Will World War III happen in days, weeks, or is it already happening? Can there be an enforceable-multinational agreement that the Climate Emergency demands actionable attention from political leaders, now? While every nation could pull together to put its efforts into saving humanity, world leaders and politicians with backwards views are acting like we have all the time in the world. Or denying the Climate Crisis exists, even when it's happening in their own backyards. Meanwhile, the world clock is ticking.

Each day a part of our minds is wondering about how to create more goodness, more caring, more compassion. Empathy. Joy. Intelligence. Shouldn't these things also be a part of this version of the future we're living in?

Building a better world should be near the top of everyone's to-do list.

Creating a better world for citizens in the US, living in a plutocracy where our healthcare system bankrupts people with dire needs, and is seen by the rest of the world as an inhumane tragedy.

The standard of living and buying power of middle-class Americans peaked in the mid-1970s. Looking at my calendar, that's a while ago. Living in a land of increasing inequality, those with less spending power are living in a society where upward mobility seems so far from current reality as to be a sick joke.
In the mid-1990s, technology shifted and was lifting more people upwards. Historical tech changes were

altering lives and upending industries. The World Wide Web was connecting the world in a way it had never been connected. Once we could go online, the effect on the working lives of people, and our ability to communicate in new ways—was life-altering on a scale previously only dreamed about.

The Internet was as culture-shifting as Gutenberg's printing press, evolving how we communicated in the span of a few years. Offering the most potent technology for globally joining humanity, it lifted spirits the way stories unfold in feel-good sci-fi movies. But the optimism and freshness of the shiny new Internet didn't hang around very long. Dystopian sci-fi themes crept into the picture. Deeply entrenched corruption grabbed hold of the Internet with big money and corrupt political power. Fast forward to 2023. A handful of social media platforms are now run by a few billionaire megalomaniacs who no longer even pretend to care about everyday people.

With the Climate Crisis now an undeniable truth and scientific reality, the voices of the young are getting louder, and more effective (no matter which alternate reality the Climate Crisis Deniers are living in). Politicians need to stop pretending business as usual will cut it during this time of crisis and transition. The same old same old won't do when multiple warring, autocratic and genocidal regimes are having a field day and our planet is already in Climate Emergency mode.

A short time ago, Greta Thunberg was a voice in the wilderness, and she's started an awakening and a growing movement. Lesson learned. Make a note of it. Showing up and doing the work can change the world. Living here and now on a Hinge of History, if this historical moment isn't the time for every voice to speak freely, when is? The question isn't why people are becoming climate activists, the question is why it took so long for it to happen.

These are historic challenges we're facing, and it's often a daily struggle to find focus. There's a time-stealing program that's been installed in our brains, continually running in the background. Wired for the quick hit of social media, distraction has stolen our focus and robbed us of our attention. Along with the ongoing pandemic, global cultural shifts, genocide, the Climate Crisis, women's rights being stolen, and book banning—we're living in an age of distraction, which has permeated every facet of our existence. Our smartphones keep us constantly connected to what's happening in real time on planet Earth. Pausing and thinking without the lies and disinformation churning in the background is a struggle. Turning down false information, and creating our own industrial-strength bullshit detectors has become a necessity.

Once upon a time the news of the world fit on three TV stations; there was a physical limit as to how much information could be delivered into your home. In the age of the 24-hour news cycle, push notifications, instant YouTube video delivery, and malignant narcissistic dictatorial world leaders, technology that we've welcomed into our lives and minds has control of us. Delivered in a daily deluge, we take in an overwhelming amount of information each day.

We're operating on a protective default setting as a safety zone around our bodies and minds. Especially when programs and platforms masquerading as news act as cultural agitators and beam propaganda into the minds of people who've slowly un-remembered what news is supposed to look and sound like, or never knew at all. The willfully misinformed commentators toss around a steady stream of lies meant to incite and antagonize like they're tossing confetti around at a private super-yacht party for a multi-billionaire.

Our deepest instincts tell us to connect to like-minded people, one's we have common interests with. People who get us. If we were constantly engaging with a passive-aggressive confrontational human being face-to-face, at some point we'd either tell them to piss off or avoid them all together. Problem solved, or at least postponed.

A constant stream of misinformation broadcast as truth is a cancer to the health of a culture. We can't forget the past, and we most definitely have to stop celebrating ignorance. If teachers aren't free to teach the truth about a country's history, as an essential understanding of why and how we've reached this point, things are so far off track we've been derailed on a frozen plain in the wilderness. If communication is broken, and opinions masquerade as truths, something's got to change.

Systemic racism has been embedded in our culture from the start, and passed down from generation to generation. This is a historical fact. Facts should be taught, and understood. History is happening all around us, at a faster pace every day. But if we don't understand and learn from the past, we're ill-prepared to deal with the multiple challenges we face during this New Now. History isn't usually pretty, and can rarely be tied with a neat little bow. The history of the world as we now experience it is in flux beyond what any of us have experienced in our lifetimes, and the immediacy of information transmission has given us unparalleled access to any horrendous or amazing event as it happens, anywhere on the planet.

People leap onto the next smartphone or the latest next generation gaming system, as a way to be tuned into the world or escape from it. But there's another side to the story. More and more people are choosing to balance their tech addictions with real life, and are gravitating in ever increasing numbers to meditation and holistic health care. It seems the more access to technology we have, the more we need to be in touch with our primal biological wiring to maintain a balance. The Internet's now being used to get people off the Internet, and guide them back to real life.

Sometimes one must find answers in the past to discover the way forward. History books are written for a reason; everyone can learn something from those who lived on this planet, whether they were here a century ago or 50 million years ago. What did our ancestors do then that'll help us now? If the new ways are doing us harm, the ancient ways might provide some much-needed wisdom.

When you're stressed out, you make worse decisions; that's a scientific fact. In a time of rampant stress-related illnesses, adding meditation to your daily routine might literally now be a life-or-death decision/prescription. A daily meditation break can literally save your life. Taking 20 minutes to sit and recharge your nervous system will rewire your brain. A walk in the woods is now doctor recommended.

There was a time when we dreamed of that happy-go-lucky Global Village when the Internet first connected us as a tool of mass communication. If you live in a part of the world where you can choose what you want to think, breathe a sigh of relief.

In this moment in history, in the most authoritarian murderous regions on the planet, it often feels like that globally interconnected village is on life support in an ICU Unit.

In the day-to-day world of living a life, people want to move freely along the sidewalk of life, feel free to love the people in their lives, make a good living, and do their part to create a more peaceful world.

A few years ago, we were isolated, asked to go into lockdown to save our own lives, and some of us saw this global reset as a pathway to a better world.

In the violence-torn Divided States of America, we wonder what happened.

Two alternate realities are competing for center stage. The state of democracy and freedom of thought, and of the press is at stake.

We must each do what makes sense to us. We can't put the genie back in the bottle and there will never be a new normal. Whatever normal life was to you, pre-pandemic, we're living in a New Now. Normal died along with the late Twentieth Century version of the American Dream. We need to rebuild, reinvent, and start anew.

As of this writing, in early 2023, the 2022 US midterms happened a few months ago, and Democrats kept control of the Senate. The Midterms were historic. Never underestimate the power of one vote. It's time to finally update what voting in a democracy means in the United States. It's time to change to a one person equals one vote system of voting, and at long last get rid of the outdated, outmoded, and especially un-democratic Electoral College.

Speaking of free and fair elections, it's time to pass a federal law to stop gerrymandering districts and let people vote knowing they're truly voting in a state that values each voter. Hiding ballot boxes and changing the voting rules from year to year on a whim is the exact wrong way to run a democracy.

A massive problem in US elections is big money. To get our political system back in good working order, the first major step is to get big billionaires and corporate money out of politics, fast. That'll go a long way to fixing our broken political system.

With historically larger voter turnouts being a part of the New Now, counting the votes accurately will become a multi-week, or month-long endeavor. Action meet reaction. Especially in a time when portable tech is so addictive some people sleep with their smartphones under their pillows (as if a futuristic Tooth Fairy will visit them as they drift off to dreamland, sending the good news of the day they desire, or gift them with the newest mobile device of their choosing.)

It's hard-wired into us to seek equality and fairness. Remember, it's not just America having problems, several other global regions are also past the tipping point. Along with cultural awakenings in Iran,

Russia, Venezuela, England, America—the social and Climate Emergency upheavals aren't going away anytime soon. This problem is bigger than all of us. It'll take a collective vision—and collaborating with love, caring, intelligence, and empathy are the only things that'll get us through this historical time period. Along with that, it'll take massive numbers of citizens voting for level-headed empathetic politicians to steer the ship of state. By not just looking for the good, but creating as much of it when we can, we'll create a better world.

A Manifesto on Manifestos

Manifestos can be written about anything under the sun, and to the far ends of the universe.

Andre Breton published *The Surrealist Manifesto* in 1924.

Frank O'Hara published *Personism: A Manifesto* in 1959.

George Maciunas published the *Fluxus Manifesto* in 1963.

Donna Haraway published *A Cyborg Manifesto* in 1985.

SARK published *How to Be an Artist* in 1989.
Bruce Mau published *An Incomplete Manifesto for Growth* in 1998.

Rick Levine, Christopher Locke, Doc Searls, and David Weinberger published *The Cluetrain Manifesto* in 2000.

Lawrence Lessig published *The Future of Ideas: The Fate of the Commons in a Connected World* in 2001.

Stephen Pressfield published *The War of Art in 2002.* Brene Brown published Daring Greatly Leadership Manifesto in 2012.

Mark Hatch published *The Maker Movement Manifesto* in 2013.

Brendon Burchard published *The Motivation Manifesto: 9 Declarations to Claim Your Personal Power* in 2014.

Tricia Hersey published *Rest is Resistance: A Manifesto* in 2022.

Manifestos about art, creativity, and all the different ways of being human have changed the world. They've shown us creative visions—poetic, surreal, and otherwise.

Fast forward to 2022: For years, domestic terrorists have written manifestos on typewriters with broken keys, and given manifestos a bad rap.

To that, we stick our fingers in our ears and say, la la la la.

Now, manifestos are for and by everyone.

Creative and quirky manifestos outnumber unhinged humans with murder in their heart's manifestos—by a large margin. Which is why you should write your own manifesto.

Write your manifesto on whatever you deeply believe in, and what you strongly care about.

By performing a quick Google search, you can find countless Manifestos.

In recent years, people have written book-length manifestos on: Motivation, Being a Lightmaker, Everyday Heroes, Menopause, Intuition, Being a Misfit, Against Ageism, Abundance, On Never Giving Up, Eating, Being Weird, Women & Politics, Gardening, Talent, Wisdom, and much more.

If there's a format of writing down what you care about that's more malleable and all-inclusive, then show us what it is.

You could write it down in a notebook (digital or paper) in 2023, and lo and behold a decade later, in 2033, you'll either want to add more life experience to it or change it entirely.

Write a manifesto to claim your place in culture, history, or even your neighborhood.

Write a manifesto in your journal and show just one person. (Even if that person is yourself.)

Write a manifesto on courage, breathing, walking, facing down your fears.

Make your mind, your heart, your body a living manifesto.

Carry around a journal that'll fit in your pocket, and collect all your powerful thoughts in it, and turn those thoughts into a manifesto for these times we're living in, surviving in, making a difference in, being uplifting when you can be, making things anew, and ultimately transforming this world for future generations.

A manifesto can be one page or hundreds of pages.

Make each day of your life a manifesto.

Write down what it's like being alive in this moment in world history—living life in this now as a student, a truck driver, a yoga instructor, a farmer, a picture framer, a teacher, a singer, a baker, a truck driver, a traveler, an artist, a philosopher—in this expanding time of continuously evolving global changes.

Put in the uniqueness of how your mind feels on the page.

This is a moment in history where everything seems possible and impossible, the end or the beginning. Each day we possess the capability of nudging the life of everyone on this planet into a better version of themselves.

We think everyone can write a manifesto. Starting as young as possible. What if kids in elementary schools were taught to write open-hearted and open-minded manifestos to counterattack the closed-minded social conditioning being heaped upon their impressionable young minds? Wouldn't that be wonderful? They could get to the saving the world part of their life story a lot quicker, with fewer mental and emotional hindrances holding them back.

The way you write your manifesto is the only way you could. It's the perfectly imperfect living document only you can make.

Words, ideas, knowledge. These things are transmitted through books. Books are mind food. Every open-hearted manifesto written in this moment in time is transmitting ideas, life, art, culture. And pointing toward a freer, more loving society.

Manifestos are the antithesis of random cleverness or street vomit. Wild words not put into a throwaway notion or random thought; manifestos are handcrafted and built upon transformative ideas and liberating visions.

A manifesto is a tool for opening minds, not a careless concept that tastes like flavorless fast food. Not made for a day news bites we consume like a lukewarm cup of take-out coffee. Manifestos are interconnected life altering ideas and visions pulled down from the sky, ideas you want to keep coming back to.

Remember to pack a journal to write your manifesto in your overnight bag.

Write a manifesto about the power of a memory you can't let go that makes you smile uncontrollably, while drinking an espresso in Sacramento.

The key to writing your manifesto is to use a good pen, one that doesn't run out of ink and writes with a flowing motion. One wonders how many brilliant ideas have been lost in time because the ink ran dry just as the ideas were flowing. If you're more of a futurist, the talk-to-text function on your phone is ideal for capturing ideas in a pinch. When you listen to them later, they'll touch your heart and grow into more expansive ideas.

Manifestos can be subversive, uplifting, funny, and as personal or global as you want them to be.

Let's pick a day, and everyone will write at least one page of a manifesto.

Write a manifesto on sensuality, musicality, and on the joy of being alive in a world where our senses interact so perfectly with it.

Create a manifesto about walking in the woods while out walking in the woods.

Each manifesto written down is a spit in the eye against mediocrity and dull sameness.

Write a manifesto from your warmly beating open heart.

How about a manifesto on loving awareness, and caring for others, and smiling when you see people holding hands and walking down the street? Manifestos about curiosity, creativity, and open-mindedness are more necessary now than ever before.

Write a manifesto about why, how, who, and what.

When you write a manifesto on paper, your thoughts are transmitted in a different way than if you'd written it on a laptop.

Write down every thought and sensation going through your mind. Edit it the next day, and turn it into a culture-shifting manifesto the day after that. Words are powerful enough to break through horrible toxic lies and restrictive thought patterns.

Manifestos open minds to what we can become, and how we can transform life for everyone on our planet—in ways no other paper or digital thought transmission tools can.

Manifestos come directly from our life experiences, and they become a record of the historical moment we're living in.

Your words and your breath are a way to change the world. Keep a journal, and within weeks your themes present themselves to you. Your manifesto will be hidden in plain sight in the journal pages you write. Write a manifesto about how words can touch peoples' hearts and save lives.

Write a manifesto about how self-censoring, by yourself or your culture is a form of senseless and cruel control. Self-censoring is lying to oneself, which must be nipped in the bud as early as possible.

Write a manifesto about the freedom to read anything, at any time, about any subject matter, written by anyone in the world.

Write a manifesto against book banning and book burning.

Never forget that words connected to ideas, minds, imaginations, and interconnected hearts can shift the culture in ways that'll make everyone on the planet sit up and take notice.

Set your alarm for 4:00 a.m. and pick up a pad of paper and a pen, then make the first word at the top of the page be: Manifesto.

Ask yourself what your deepest core message would be if you were to begin writing your manifesto here and now.

Write a manifesto on scraps of paper you find in your apartment, or on park benches.

Begin a manifesto that'll take you a year, a decade, half a century to write.

Write a manifesto on the kind of world you want to live in.

America has a book banning problem

"I had thought America was against totalitarianisms. If so, surely it is important for young people to be able to recognize the signs of them. One of those signs is book-banning. Need I say more?"

– **Margaret Atwood**, responding to news of her books being banned in Leander, Texas

From banning books by Walt Whitman to Allen Ginsberg, and from Toni Morrison to Margaret Atwood—there's a long history of hysteria and authoritarianism around preventing books that will open minds and change hearts from getting into the hands of readers in America.

This week is National Library Week. Which makes one think of book bans, and why they've become so prevalent. Another sign of the country gone mad with authoritarians trying to take more and more rights away?

PEN America has put out this short list of some of the most recent banned books titles:

Gender Queer: A Memoir by Maia Kobabe
All Boys Aren't Blue by George M. Johnson
Lawn Boy by Jonathan Evison
Out of Darkness by Ashley Hope Pérez
The Bluest Eye by Toni Morrison
Beyond Magenta: Transgender Teens Speak Out by Susan Kuklin

The fact that Toni Morrison, one of the greatest writers this country has ever had is on this list is an American tragedy. The fact that any of these books are on a banned book list in this country, in the year 2023 is an American tragedy.

The book banning across the United States, that's accelerated year by year is one step away from book burning, and is a national disgrace.

Groups demanding that books be restricted or removed from libraries in the United States rose by 38% in 2022.

Removing books from school and public libraries is undemocratic thought control.

Where is the right for freedom of choice, freedom of thought, freedom of curiosity for every reader, in 2023?

Most books bans are put in place to stop students from their right to read freely, by organizations whose sole purpose is banning books, censoring books, keeping books deemed inappropriate reading matter—due to LGBTQ+ themes or characters, people of color as the main protagonist, books that directly deal with racism, books containing any form of sexual experiences or relationships conveying sexuality, and anything to do with activism and standing up for one's rights.

In other words, teenagers need to be protected from the regular course of being curious and alive in the world.

If you're against reading freely and liberally, natural curiosity, a far-ranging interest in knowledge, you're doing nothing but trying to turn the culture backwards, and that's not going to work.

Trying to remove any trace of LGBTQ+ books, and any books with characters confronting race/racism in today's world? Have you thought about how impossible this is?

If your goal is to stop kids from getting titles they want to read, and prevent them from getting a copy in their school library, or local public library, there's this thing called the Internet, and most cities still have bookstores you can walk into and buy books.

The majority of citizens in the United States are against book banning.

School libraries are being attacked by far-right organizations with blocking freedom of thought as their main goal.

Books that reflect characters like themselves back to a student could save or change their life.

Previously, they could easily find such a book at their school library, or their local library.

If physical books are being banned in their city, town, county, or state, students do have an eBook choice at their fingertips.

In response to books being censored and librarians and authors being silenced across the country, the Brooklyn Public Library started Books Unbanned. Students anywhere in the United States between the ages of 13 and 21 are invited to apply for a free Brooklyn Public Library (BPL) eCard.

Open your mind to the ideas you are interested in knowing more about.

Like all art, books save lives.

Stories where a reader recognizes themselves are life-saving stories.

Banning these types of diverse and inclusionary books is unconscionable.

From Seattle to Brooklyn, public libraries have stood up against book banning

"This land is your land, this land is my land, from California to the New York island…"
– **Woody Guthrie**

Along with The Brooklyn Public Library, The Seattle Public Library has stood up for the right to read freely, and against those who censor your thoughts by banning books.

From coast to coast, it's easier than ever to read banned books and open your mind.

It's a proven fact: Books free your mind.
Suppressing democracy and freedom of thought
is wrong.

If you're a teen or young adult from 13 to 26, and
live anywhere in the United States, sign up for a free
Books Unbanned card and read whatever interests
you. With a Books Unbanned library card, you can
check out from both libraries' online collections of
e-books and e-audiobooks.

If your school or local public library is under attack,
and extremist authoritarians are busy trying to
prevent you from reading any book you want to read,
you can sign up for a free Books Unbanned library
card, either from the Seattle Public Library or the
Brooklyn Public Library.

In early May 2023 the Illinois Senate has become
the first state to ban book bans. Weeks later, the
Democratic Governor then signed it into law. This is
book banning resistance at its best.

Minds open up to new ideas through the power of
reading. No one has the right to take this fundamental
freedom away.

No one has the right to prevent free thought in
a democracy.

Those who want to restrict the right to freely access ideas contained in books are on the wrong side of history.

Anyone who wants to take away the right to read freely is promoting an un-American idea.

Access to a diversity of ideas and information, is especially essential on the most often banned types of books—LGBTQ+ and books with people of color as the main character in a story.

Extremist groups are attempting to remove the right to read freely.

There's a wonderful feeling in finding an author who feels like they know you.

Any book that reflects your life experience back to you, serves to open your mind, and helps you to clearly see your personal truth, is a good book.

Read what you enjoy reading. This can literally be anything you're deeply drawn to.

Minds are meant to be opened up, not closed down.

Read anything and everything about the world, nature, books, art, people, music, love, creativity, science, and most importantly of all, yourself.

Walt Whitman's Leaves of Grass, when first published, was considered too shocking in its poems about sexuality, including same-sex relationships.

In 1855, Ralph Waldo Emerson wrote this to Walt Whitman, after Whitman had sent Emerson a copy of Leaves of Grass.

"I greet you at the beginning of a great career, which yet must have had a long foreground somewhere, for such a start. I rubbed my eyes a little, to see if this sunbeam were no illusion; but the solid sense of the book is a sober certainty. It has the best merits, namely, of fortifying and encouraging."

A District Attorney in Boston, banned sales of the newly published 1882 sixth edition, considering Leave of Grass "obscene." Whitman refused to take out the words and passages that offended the DA.

Whitman's writing voice seems as clear to a modern reader as if he wrote it last week.

Section 51, Song of Myself

Do I contradict myself?

Very well then I contradict myself,

(I am large, I contain multitudes.)

Now considered one of the greatest books ever
written in America, Leaves of Grass has been read
widely throughout the world, and influenced writers
and artists such as Bob Dylan, Allen Ginsberg, and
Charles Bukowski.

Living in the Divided States of America

It's now unmistakable. We're living in two separate countries.

There's an uneasy feeling across the land. For some time, we've sensed that we're already in a Civil War, and it began years ago.

It's now unmistakable. We're living in two separate countries.

We're in a time when agreement on most levels with certain people just isn't going to happen.

A vocal minority wants an autocratic system (some of them desire a theocratic system) of governance where the dictator-in-charge will ban free thought and diversity, being able to believe what you want to believe, and live life with as much freedom as you can.

On the subject of authoritarians and would-be dictators, some people are mesmerized by these grifters and con men and could bathe in their lies forevermore. But, those who saw through the barrage of lies from the start just want to turn off the faucet of flimsy deceits forever.

We watched the exact same person and the despicable actions he performed, the exact same violent events that happened live on TV, and the exact same detailed broadcast of factual information about those events talked about daily for months. These historic events were seen through personal, societal, and cultural lenses so far apart as to be light years away from each other.

We aren't in a let's ignore all these relentless untruths, stolen rights, and horrific violence type of mood.

History and reality has shown that those on the left side of the political divide didn't attempt to overthrow America with a violent insurrection. Only a matter of months ago. History books (if we're lucky) will show this too.

We're living in two separate countries. It's unmistakable.

If you haven't already changed your mind about the guy who used to go to the oval office and mostly grunt grievances, for the entirety of his time in office, no longer sure what it'll take. Oh wait, he was just indicted again, in early June 2023. This time it's for multiple federal felonies. It's a long list, but one of the top felonies he's been charged with is Willful Retention of National Defense Information, which is concerned with putting the security of our country at risk. Something we should all be concerned with?

We're living in a time when both sides aren't going to agree about much of anything. Maybe partly agree on some fundamentals. As long as it's not extremist fundamentalism.

Hopefully we can agree finally, finally, finally, to legislate and enforce laws that'll stop the ongoing senseless gun violence that's affected every group of people in the country, but is especially targeted at kids, black people, Asian people, and LGBTQ+

people. That a lot of hate-filled, murderous hearts, with easy access to powerful weapons of war. Senseless, horrific violence continues happening week by week, with a steady drip, drip, drip, of murder, bullets, blood, and tears.

Enough is enough. Pass stronger federal gun control laws.

One school shooting after another, where young people are literally slaughtered by a person using a weapon of war, and once more only hearing thoughts and prayers.

Thoughts and prayers. These often-spoken words ring hollow. They don't mean it. We don't want to hear it. If those words ever carried any meaning, they sure don't now.

May someday we know actual truth when it continually bites us on the ass.

In 2010, the Supreme Court told us with their Citizens United decision that corporations are people. In reality, what this means is that corporations can buy elections. Clear enough?

Corporations are run by people, but a corporate entity is NOT a person. There's that pesky reality part of things showing up again.

When free speech costs billions, suddenly it isn't so free anymore.

When people with gay kids are forced to move out of Florida, that's coming from disgusting policies and awful autocratic behavior. How many people know someone who has moved their family out of the United States due to the horrific weekly gun violence? Constant carnage. Weekly mass shootings. How did it come to this?

In early June 2023, The Human Rights Campaign has declared a national state of emergency for LGBTQ+ citizens across the United States. This is literally saying, it's not safe anywhere in the nation for gay people. How did we reach this increasingly awful point as a nation?

It's now unmistakable. We're living in two separate countries.

When writing down what should be manifestly clear and based on true events is controversial, one has to ask, how did we get to this point?

Of course, there are other forms of reality, in the form of cosmic dimensions and metaverses, and for day-to-day life, there are connections and conversations and having breakfast, and watching the morning news explode from the TV set. There's morning coffee and dinnertime discussions, and taking the dog for a walk. But, all of this happens while the propaganda channel broadcasts nothing remotely true in the background.

We've experienced enough gaslighting as a form of societal control. We've tuned out the insane level of gaslighting going on. When nothing's true everything is true. When reality is up for debate, hold onto your hat. Don't look over there. Keep your curiosity to a minimum. Don't ask too many questions. Stay in line. How did we reach this point?

We're not listening anymore. Your attempts at authoritarianism didn't work. We've seen through your act. You are terrible at lying.

If some of us welcome autocrats and authoritarianism, then we must ask why. Authoritarians want to eradicate those who don't comply with their bloodthirsty need to dominate and destroy. History doesn't lie. Go online or pick up a book. The entire history of Civilization is there for you to dive into. It shows us again and again what will return if we let it. Dictatorships. Fascism. Autocracies. Totalitarian regimes. These don't sound like good forms of governments to live under, do they? Emphasis on the word under.

Countless studies have shown more and more Americans consider themselves spiritual but not religious. I wonder why. Thoughts and prayers? It keeps coming back to our individual choices, and the choices made for us behind closed doors. Bad legal decisions that affect everyone, decided by corrupt people.

Wasn't the future supposed to be a friendlier place? Smarter than ever before? We were told there would be robots for all, and we'd be flying on highways in the sky. Made for everyone, and not just the ultra-wealthy?

Earlier each year, wildfire seasons are creating unbreathable air, more and more toxic to humans. Seattle was closed down for a week a few summers ago. It was too dangerous to go outdoors and breathe. In June, 2023, New York City and London experienced Climate Crisis related toxic air quality events.

How did we reach this point in 2023?

It seems breathable air is necessary for all humans, even if you're an authoritarian or a billionaire.

What will it take to create a better world for all of us?

Digital Fire: A Manifesto

Welcome to the Age of Reinvention, we've been expecting you

When in the course of human events—a new planetary movement springs up and connects all societies—it becomes self-evident that the time has come to fully embrace reinvention for the purpose of survival. It's time to engage in true passionate creativity, and all that follows from asking more of ourselves, our lives, our minds and hearts, our cultures, governments, organizations and institutions—every single day.

Mark it on your Google calendar and ink it on your wall calendar. Draw it in the dirt and write it on the sky with an airplane or a magic marker. Scribble it in a notebook or YouTube it to the masses. Text it, email it, blog it, video chat it, and yell it in the streets. Write it on a cave wall or graffiti it on a brick wall in the heart of the city. The Age of Reinvention has arrived.

Wonderful, tragic, and cataclysmic events have unfolded in recent days, months, and years. Every person on Earth has been impacted. Societies, countries, and cultures have all begun spiraling in a new direction—a direction with no less an end result than altering the history of the human race. Interconnected through technology, we've grown new minds and new spines, and we can no longer afford to live stagnant unsurprising lives.

People everywhere now know that open minds and engaged humans are the minds and people of the future. Now is the time for free thought and freethinkers. If the current version of our future isn't teaching us lessons of urgency and ingenuity, and we aren't at our core already reinventing ourselves, we're on the wrong screen and need to quickly swipe away, and find the screen showing this crucial idea and vital way forward.

Reinvent or crawl back under your covers for a decades-long nap. Set your alarm for a century into the future. Rethink where you are, what you can accomplish, and how you present yourself to every person you come in contact with. Reinsert yourself into the digital flow and join your life already in progress. Renew how your perception, beliefs, and essence of being shape your interactions with the people of this world. Reshape thoughts into organic devices able to pinpoint and communicate with a human being on the opposite side of the planet, blasting through language barriers and cultural walls, and getting directly to the point of being alive in our historical moment.

Instantaneously connecting via text, email, or Zoom—has brought citizens of Earth closer together, and a perfectly imperfect organic change movement was made possible through our devices. Worldwide connections are made. The fuse is lit. Live, immediate transmissions from zones of pain, power, protest, disaster have been broadcast and assimilated. Either by evolving into the New Now, or pushed by dire circumstances, more people on the planet know they want a fundamental shift to happen in their lives. Stories were sent from far flung locations, old and new media intermingled and keep intermingling. The Digital Everywhere was created by necessity. Our planet required it. If you are engaged, alert, and feel a growing spark inside—you're open to the idea of reinvention happening on a global scale. Welcome to this precise moment. We've been expecting you.

Digital communication devices are accessible to people in the most remote corners of the planet. Reinvention is within their grasp, touchpad, keypad, mobile device. Connect and aspire—inspire, and feel the digital fire. The reinvention of getting the word out is complete, languages have been decoded, and everyone's ideas about everything are being transmitted and are freely encircling the globe.

Imagine if the Declaration of Independence were written on a laptop and emailed to world leaders, kings, and tyrants as soon as the virtual ink dried. What if smartphones had been in use during the Salem Witch trials? Candid powdered wig photos showing twisted grimaces of those who murdered out of fear and ignorance. Strange goings on would have abounded; voices, images, and mapped locations sent by an unknown being from another time and place, crossing through the time barrier. With your magical device recording the deaths hanging in the air, they'd suspect you were in league with dark forces, and being hanged or burned at the stake would be in your immediate future. Now, these devices are uncovering and upending murderous regimes in our current times. Look around. Revolutions are not televised as Gil Scott-Heron predicted in song, but uploaded to the instantaneous Internet in real time.

Freethinkers and open-minded dreamers are giving the world a new spin. Just as in past centuries, freethinkers are permanently altering the future. As if they've been beamed in from our own future, they've arrived. Right on time. Ready to travel the globe or wander through a neighborhood, altering history as they go. Sending out warnings and visions of change. Look around. They're sitting next to you in your local coffee shop or bar. Feel free to interact with them. Two people can now start a movement. It's not just allowed, it's encouraged. Creating life-altering change through exchanging ideas is a fundamental wonderful expectation. It's now expected you're here to change the world for the better.

We are living in an expansive moment in world history. Societies are being turned inside-out. Rethink the way you perceive and operate in the natural and digital world. Hearts and minds are being rewired—from continent to continent and pole to pole. Take a breath; feel it to be the real truth. The internal architecture of our brains is being rebuilt. Reinvention has been established as a primary goal for billions of people.

Reinvention isn't a commodity. It's a quantum idea, a miraculous meme, a fluid structure, a new set of eyes, a path forward. People have hit a wall, and they realize it's time to either knock through it, crawl over it, levitate higher than the tallest building, or just open their eyes to a world where walls only serve to unite, not divide. A wall with holes in it allows vines and curving stems holding flowers to reach over to the other side.

Reinvention asks everything of you, and it asks nothing of you. You can join the reinvention movement from anywhere on the globe. It's up to each person to rethink thinking and renew their being. The dumbing down of cultures and citizens is a tragedy that must be reversed. Words, language, ideas, and reading many books is a superpower. Dive into the deep end of the ocean of knowledge. Every book, and every type of book is a miracle. The intellectual erosion of humanity has already gone too far. There are countless books, and millions and millions of them are good books. And there arc new words and thoughts commingling and changing minds, younger and older.

Minds with accumulated celebratory creative wisdom in them are needed to get us through the near future and into the new future. Smart must be the new strong, the new belief system, the way of living life in the New Now. Think. Think of new ways to be, do, act, live.

The future has arrived. We are living in the Age of Reinvention.

Manifesto #2: Welcome to the New Now

We are the people who will decide the future of our planet

It's happening again. Life is changing. People, younger and older, friendly or fearful, vibrant or forlorn, intently focused, or nodding out while walking down the street of life—all feel global tectonic cultural shifts going on around them and rumbling through them. Look around. We're standing in the historical river of history. And the flood waters are rising.

We are here to save the planet. We're all now makers, creators, builders, and the people who will remake and reinvent our lives, which will propel us forward into a New Now.

Looking at the changing world we live in, we each ask ourselves what really matters. The future is calling us forward, and some of us are taking steps to rebuild how everything works and to create a new sustainable world.

Intent on keeping humanity human, we're feeling expansive and ready for the adventures and challenges ahead. Along the way, we're each building our own answers from the ground up. Reinventing our lives and our culture.

As we're pulled deeper into the century stretching out before us, we're heading into an uncharted land of transformative social and technical experiences at a time of challenge, renewal, and reinvention. We've learned the hard way that the best minds and hearts must lead a nation. Loving kindness matters, and it can change the course of history. It's time to radiate out love. A jolt of love energy to the entire social ecosystem will alter everything in an instant.

The experiential nature of living in the New Now is altering everyone on the planet. At an accelerated pace, there's a rebirth of creating and a new joy about making things, reinventing things, and completely rebuilding our dysfunctional and damaging social systems. No person or place has been untouched, and everyone has a say. Tattoo it on your skin or frontal lobe: We Are All Creators. The creative force lives within our cells and organs. Voices are rising up. We are saying it in larger numbers every day, and speaking up with strength and unity. Amidst the chaos, dying, and destruction—fresh flowers are rising up from the earth.

One day, not so long ago, communication devices began appearing in our hands and on our heads. As if by magic the interconnectivity communication devices were deployed—over time, even more transformative technological leaps have promised to make us newer, shinier versions of ourselves. All made to enhance communication, to each other, and to our living environments. Along the way, we've discovered that tech without heart rings hollow, like thumping on the Tin Man's chest. Leaders in technology and media have claimed this era as the Digital Age, but a more accurate name for the times we're living through is the Age of Reinvention.

In the Age of Reinvention, whole societies and individual lives are being re-envisioned, restructured, rebooted. As our cities and societies crumble and rise again, new ways of living and interacting are waiting in the wings, ready to be switched on. New minds have been installed. Science has shown us we can rewire and transform our own brain, in the same way Artificial Intelligence has just made a quantum leap forward, quantum computing is just around the corner. Time and space will be overcome and readjusted to reflect our new minds and new spines, and we'll continue to adapt to the recurring tsunamis of environmental, societal, cultural, and global disasters and challenges.

We're living in a time when being stuck in the past is a form of death. Living inside each day, we count experiences, ideas, emotions as they pass through us. Years accumulate and roll through our memories like pages flipping in books. Decades flow through our lives and we become more aware of how we fit into the changing world around us. In this New Now, we require visionaries, makers, poets, musicians, scientists, empaths, artists builders, and culture shifters in every field.

Learning from the past and time traveling through books, films, musical artifacts is a wonder and a gift. Accessing the historical brilliance of creative spirits compels us forward. But living in a cyclical past of repeating mistakes over and over isn't sustainable, for a person or a culture. It's time for each of us to create in the world of possibilities. Without hesitating and without giving into fear or willful ignorance—we're remaking how we interact with each other while reinventing art, work, relationships, love, architecture, social systems, cities, bodies, food supplies, water sources, and modes of communication.

Being alive now is unlike being alive in earlier, unconnected centuries. The ecosystem of the planet is speaking to each of us. In shouts, cries, and whispers. At the same time, technology is morphing and mutating all of us. Speaking to us and transforming us in countless ways. New creative strands of DNA deep within each of us have been switched on. Nature is grabbing us by the collar and hollering into our ear-budded ears. We've opened digital doorways with our minds, and activated dormant survival systems that've been waiting millennia to be turned on. The New Now supports and believes in more social acceptance for everyone. Sad, it actually still needs to be said. Yes, we're all one, and truly in this together.

With economic and technological disruption have come freedom, creativity, and chaos. People can experience all the effects of these three states of mind in one day, or in an hour of their lives. Dive into the creative flow state to make what you're called to make, and become who you must become. Making personal changes centered on creativity and flow has become a universal imperative. Choosing our own essential imperative is included in the digital code that's already melded with our biological code. Freedom and wonder have leapt off the screen and live on city streets, nearby oceans, and high on mountaintops.

In the Age of Reinvention, people have become more of who they were meant to be. There's no hiding in caves of the mind anymore and there's no reason to waste time. Time's always been the great leveler. Now it is both the most important thing on the planet, and the most expansive and expensive thing around. Time turns on a dime and is worth billions. Time is free when you choose it to be. We've come face to face with time in generation-defining ways. Time is a renewable commodity carried around in invisible luggage. Time is what's closest to our hearts and at the center of our being. Time can be an open door to forever when you're in a flow state, or it can be a boulder crushing your spirit when you're a bundle of suffering. It's time for each of us to take back our internal clocks and redefine the meaning of time for ourselves.

Digital information surrounds us, chases after us, and forces us to be wiser curators of our own minds/lives. New Now and future generations will never have known a world where the Internet, smartphones, global pandemics, streaming media, a global climate emergency, AI, digital devices, clones, drones, robots, and all that's yet to be imagined didn't exist. Buckminster Fuller's Spaceship Earth and Marshall McLuhan's Global Village have become reality—not in a faraway future, but here and now in the early decades of the twenty-first century. The past and our future-to-be have collided and intersected, asking only one thing of us. Everything.

In the Age of Reinvention real human interaction is primary. Which isn't to say new modes of being present and traveling through time and space are out of the question; someone has to eventually invent the time machine. As we travel deeper into the multiverse of Artificial Intelligence, rewiring our brains will be taught in grade schools. Connectivity and community may begin online, but people are hardwired to read faces, communicate ideas, collaborate on projects, and make significant and lasting changes together.

The Age of Reinvention has begun, and what we do with this expanded sense of connectivity and creativity is up to each of us.

Manifesto #3:
Reinvent You

If not now, when?

You can rewire your brain, and reinvent yourself. Download and install the new programs you've chosen. Neuroscience has proven it's possible. If you want to, you can alter your mind—with words, thoughts, feelings, and visions of your own choosing. Rewiring your brain is a day-by-day process. Using stillness and new thought patterns, you can overwrite the past and alter your future. Now, it's time to begin what you've always wanted to begin.

It's possible to start creating the New Now you've wanted for years, decades, or even longer. If you want it passionately enough, you only need to ask yourself one question. If not now, when?

Creating a New Now begins with trying out new ideas. Then seeing which ones resonate with you. Reinvention changes your life. Just about everyone is trying to change their life in some way. You want to feel better, and wake up with new eyes of surprise. The world wants our lives to be renewed, revived, and reinvigorated. Reinvention is as necessary as breathing fresh air, drinking clean water, and taking walks in nature. It's time to rewire and recharge your brain, body, spirit. Listen to your intuition. Reaching up to the next level is your daily human project. Reinvention has become one of the main life-altering ideas changing lives in our culture. Now it's a part of the life and death decisions centered around how people live, grow, interact, and survive. Recently, survival mode was turned on and fully functioning. Sometimes history comes along and makes adapting to drastic changes a part of everyday life. We now know how other historical and prehistoric events happened. Goodbye dinosaurs; Hello Black Death; So long, Hunter and Gatherers; Greetings fall of the Berlin Wall. In a matter of days or weeks, the lives of countless humans and creatures were transformed.

Prehistory turned into history. Yesterday turned into today.

In the blink of billions of eyes, we've transitioned from the Digital Age to the Age of Reinvention. Coming along shortly, the Age of Light and Freedom. Everyone has begun rewiring their brains, using thought patterns, ideas, and creative flow. More intuitive modes of communication are now a high priority since it's a matter of eco-planetary and human survival.

Reinvention is about changing the course of how we respond to hard pressing realities like facing the worldwide humanity-made global Climate Crisis, and the massive cultural shift of a multi-year global pandemic. In an ongoing reality touching every life on the planet, we're all massively transforming. To debate this fact is like debating whether the sun will rise tomorrow, or if the wind will push clouds across the sky. In this New Now, the reinvention of one's way of doing and being has become a necessity.

Inventors, creatives, builders, investors, makers, scientists, architects, planters, organizers, healers, visionaries—working together must combine their talents on a global scale never attempted before—to fundamentally repair our damaged world, and our broken social systems. To fix things with hands and hearts, the way they used to be fixed. Global unity must no longer be a faraway pipe dream; it's time for us to become melded together in the New Now.

Overheard on a street corner in Seattle: "It all started with two people in a room." It could just as well have been: "It all started with two people on a houseboat." Likewise: "It all started with two people in a garage." Ideas exchanged with excitement and clarity are powerful tools. We've used these mind tools to arrive here, while our devices transmit instantaneous communications.

Two people in a room, a basement, or a garage, aligned with dozens of humans in thousands of rooms, have reinvented the way people communicate, build relationships, and relay information. Fast forward to anywhere on the globe. Five out of five people sitting on a subway car or a city bus (or in the near future, a high-speed rail) are staring down at a smarter smartphone mobile device in their hand. Each looking at different versions of our world. Our world in turmoil and transition. And of course, along the way we feel sparks of joy and laughter—which makes each of us understand better who we are inside. Everyone interprets life according to what makes them glow inside.

The Internet gave us the Digital Age. The Digital
Age gave birth to the Mobile World. The Mobile
World is connected to your agile moving fingers, and
has spawned the Imaginative Digital Everywhere.
Everything we experience in the form of streaming
movies, music, talks, podcasts—all of it—everything
digitized and moving invisibly through the air
started from ideas, connections, collaborations,
and creations. Across the globe, the Imaginative
Digital Everywhere transforms, excites, blends
with our rapidly evolving human minds. Cultural
transformations can't be held back. Reinvented minds
open cultures, like they're supposed to do.
Reinvention is about becoming who you've wanted
to be all along, and becoming who you're supposed
to be, according to you. For the purpose of self-
evolving, you are your one and only authority.

Reinvention is a choice you make on your own. This
is not to say you do it all alone. Nothing is done
without ideas reacting to ideas that came before. The
trick is to be tuned into ideas that excite you and
resonate in the deepest core of your being. Whether
heard in conversations, viewed on video screens, or
found in books—ideas shift cultures.

For decades now—people, companies, organizations,
have all claimed to be reinventing themselves, or

talked about the need to reinvent themselves. Some people talk a lot and produce no actions. Some actions pretend to possess meaning. Avoid endless circular meetings about nothing for the sake of your sanity and move toward the opposite. Seek out gatherings and events with people seeking the creative loving world of the New Now. Meet in the place where two people with ideas talk and put dreams down on paper and then use ideas to change the world. Write it down, and then make it happen.

We built and shaped technology, and it's shaped us. We need to re-regulate our beings. It's time to fully reset ourselves: mind, body, and spirit.

Now we're relearning the art of slowing down and pausing. Deeply altering who we are inside, we've slowed almost to a stopping point, so that we may begin again as the version of ourselves we've been envisioning for years. Scroll down the menu, and choose your selection from the Imaginative Digital Everywhere for the type of life you want. Pause and pick up a pen and a notebook. A pen you like the feel of in your hand, and a notebook with paper pages. Physicality matters. Write down your own pathway ahead through our changing world. Become a dreamer who is also a doer.

People have re-re-re-discovered how "aware stillness" is more important than "distracted busyness." It's common knowledge how the mind delivers answers when you let it rest in nature. Culture shifting ideas come to you during those times when you are out walking, staring up at the ceiling, or just sitting on a park bench.

Reinvention often begins with asking the right questions. Question the accepted truths of your culture (which have long become irrelevant). Question your own questions. Question every accepted cultural norm. Question why you've been stuck in the past. Question why things are the way they are, and how we got to this point. It's connecting to different types of people that want to stir things up, change how things have always been done, that makes where we are in history so amazingly interesting.

People are waking up to the life-changing reality of making drastic changes to create the future world humanity will live in.

It would be amazing to possess the ability to zip ahead a few hundred years in the future and see how we made it through our current worldwide crisis mode, and developed into smarter, wiser, more intuitive, more freethinking, and more tolerant human beings.

In the meantime, we can envision this improved and wondrous future, and can make it with our minds. Which is the exact way everything has ever gotten made in this world. Reinvention is a form of time travel. It allows you to change yourself step by step, week by week. It's your choice. By changing one aspect of your life, in a year, you've reinvented a large part of your life. You knew what you wanted to create, and you reached for it through time. First you envision, then you grasp onto reality. You were pulled forward by your own future, and these transformations were created by your own effort.

Welcome to the New Now. You've been expecting you.

Manifesto #4 /
A Manifesto for Creativity

Beginning again in the New Now

Take a breath.

Now's the time for every type of new beginning imaginable.

The beginning you planned for and expected, and the one that blindsided you and left your vision blurry for a time. The beginning that's so different it's like living in a dream. The beginning you had stashed away in your secret cupboard.

Each day begins in the same way and in a different way. It's up to you to choose.

Imagine a beginning that feels like the best start of the best morning you can remember.

Write. Dance. Paint. Cook. Make tea. Meditate. Talk. Organize a Zoom meeting. Garden. Sew. Hum to yourself. Do yoga. Take a long walk. In whichever way your creative energy has led you, it's taken you to this moment where we're all living in this place called now.

Strange times, we all sigh, and say. And then we begin again.

All days begin, somehow, and someplace. Sometimes the same place. A place you've grown to know and love. Maybe you're in a new place, a place that's helped create good memories for many who arrived there before you.

All creative projects begin by just beginning. It starts by making a mark on a page. Then making yourself into who you want to be.

How do you read a book? By scanning words and lines, and turning pages. Books are time machines, doorways to other worlds, and a perfect restful room to visit and reprogram your mind.

Every song, movie, novel, or play had to have a beginning. It started on one particular day. A single day out of a lifetime. Focused minds and hearts have created like this from the start, before there were words—only gestures and grunts, and a cave wall to paint on.

In our modern world, before the New Now, the time to create was usually carved out of a life. Grabbing a few hours here and there. Returning to a painting. Adding several paragraphs to a book.

Now, things are different. We're awakening from transition mode. The whole world is coming back from being put on pause.

Something history-altering came along, and time was expanded. Here we are. We've lived through an expansive historical moment. How often do these come along? A global event true for everyone at the exact same time. Have at it, creators.

Remember, we are all wired to create. And remember this—we all want to feel better, and feel lighter inside. One of the best reasons to perform a creative act is how it makes you feel. It's the feeling of time stopping, or expanding, or being in a space where time doesn't exist. It's how you feel being in the flow state.

Creativity loves the flow state of being. One of the experiences creatives access each time they move into the flow state, is the wonderful feeling of time stopping.

How does it feel for you? Being in the state of timelessness, and often feeling lighter inside. The creative experience flows in two directions. Inward and outward. Like the everyday miracle of breathing.

We are at our best when we are present in the world, with ourselves or others.

If you feel stuck in the past, the unstuck pills are freely available, inside your mind. Take an imaginary pill for the imagination, and pick up a pencil, paintbrush, hammer, camera, or guitar. Begin making something.

It also begins further back, when you first saw a piece of art that made your brain tingle. How you felt when you experienced the very first movie that delighted and overwhelmed you as a child. How you felt when you were a bit older, and you heard a new song on the radio, or discovered how amazingly some buildings were shaped, or you were sitting with a crowd of people in a basement, and you listened to a poet read their poems aloud for the first time.

All of these experiences, people, places, had a beginning.

Turning creativity on by taking action is how it's always been done.

See yourself picking up a pair of scissors, a musical instrument, or a paintbrush. Picture yourself pushing notes out into the air with your breath, or placing colors on a canvas.

Feel yourself making something destined to change how someone's feeling.

Imagine making something to shift your culture forward. Envision creating a song, or a painting, or a character in a movie that will completely transform the world.

In creative flow, as in this historical moment, you don't yet know how it's going to turn out.

Take a breath, and pick up a journal. Capture your thoughts.

Take a walk. To the park across the street. To the hillside five miles away. To the spot calling you in a dream.

Look at the birds flying high above your head, and walking near your feet. The loudly shouting crows and the cheeping flitting little birds who live in the bushes.

See the world with fresh eyes. Do it again and again. Ideas often come to you when you're wandering around your city, or in a new town you've never been in before.

Open up to possibilities. Your mind will thank you later.

Creating is individual. Creating is collaborative.

Creating is imagination plus action. Creating is necessary. Creating can be timeless and weightless.

Art saves lives and expands how you experience the world.

Being open to wonder is a portal to many other states of being.

Songs and movies have changed peoples' lives. When the words in a song, or the emotions in a performance resonate deeply inside someone, they indeed changed the direction of a life—and art did what it's supposed to do.

Envisioning it leads to doing it.

Some days call for small steps, and other days ask for you to get on a rocket ship to Jupiter.

You get to figure out which type of day you're making for yourself.

Start today. Begin making something in this moment. It can be anything.

It's time to create what you want to create.

If not now, when?

A Declaration of Interdependence #1

We the People declare we're living at a turning point in history, and we decided to change history.

We the People declare we deserve a transparent, fully functioning, thriving Democracy. It's pretty much what the Founders promised, in writing.

We the People declare we didn't expect to live in a time when Reality itself needs our protection. Yet here we are.

We the People declare it is way past time to create a more perfect union.

We the People declare, so it appears there really were space aliens visiting Earth, and science fiction novels were sending us secret coded messages all along.

We the People declare being on the right side of history is about being open-minded, and respecting freedom of thought and of the press.

We the People declare making a new way and a new day begins with open and truthful communications.

We the People declare we wholeheartedly believe in commonsense solutions that benefit everyone.

We the People declare an end to blind and foolish hatred, in every corner of the world. Every human being now gets to believe what they want to believe and become who they want to become.

We the People declare it's time to exhale toxic social conditioning and brainwashing.

We the People declare it's a brand-new day.

We the People declare it's time to stand up for core humanistic values.

We the People declare, there are infinite possibilities for shifting our culture. Choose one and work toward making it happen.

We the People declare there's no time like the present.

We the People declare we've seen the future, and closed-minded fools have no place in it.

We the People declare we're ready like we've never been ready before.

We the People declare we're intelligent, informed, and perceptive enough to understand we are living through the first stages of an Ecological Apocalypse.

We the People declare many of us have found a way forward, through the dimly lit tunnel, and beyond the tangled bramble of endless disinformation.

We the People declare we love how seeing everything with clarity makes it all worthwhile.

We the People declare: And the children shall lead them.

We the People declare on some nights we are as high as the sky and over the moon.

We the People declare everything is now pointed in the best possible direction.

We the People declare we are overjoyed at how everywhere youth have risen up and begun a worldwide movement for Environmental, Social, and Political Change. The children have stars in their eyes, and are immune to often repeated lies.

We the People declare the arc of history has enfolded all of us into its expansive and ongoing narrative, and we're now officially along for the ride. Historians will figure it out and untangle it a hundred years from now.

We the People declare momentum, mystery, and history are all on our side.

We the People can see a new way of living with our wide-open eyes, and it's just over the next hill.

Manifesto # 5 / Preamble to a Cultural and Social Renaissance

On the far shore of somewhere new

We the People of the United States of Somewhere New, are now getting back to the business and pleasure of forming a more perfect union, all the while realizing we're perfectly imperfect beings having a human experience, just as the Cosmos, Nature, and the Muses of Creativity intended.

Whatever else may happen, it's time to create a cultural and social renaissance, based on love and communication and taking care of each other, by making art, music, writing—while adding empathy and intuition and loving kindness into the mix. Moving it all ahead on sidewalks, and freeways, in loft spaces, and along wooded paths. With understanding, respect, and open-hearted wonder, our world can be remade.

In our less-than-tranquil times, where invisible threats and societal strife and fear abounds, we'll carve out the means to be less mean and making what matters, in every way possible.

We want new stories full of infinite surprise, and music full of heart-centered joy. We want to feel release and relief, and to laugh up at the stars. Whether it's making a living, or making music, or making art, or making love, or making movies, or making a point—doing it with open hearts leads to a higher level of doing it.

Creation comes in many forms, and it likes it like that. On the far shore of Somewhere New, we've got to get things going again, as we've always done before. Before this moment. Here in the New Now.

Where do we go from here? True to form, new forms made out of truth and clarity are established every time something false and wrong is normalized in a culture. As it was before, it will be again. The pendulum is swinging back toward the light. We're turning away from lies, disinformation, and darkness. Our current cultural forms need reinventing and expanding upon. By whom? All those who said no to doing nothing, and yes to creating. How about changing the future? How about transforming a neighborhood garden? How about building a house of clouds from the ground up?

Nature has surprised us, and thrown us to the ground in a way we've never experienced before. And now we must rediscover new ways of being. Some of these were buried by cultural conditioning. Some have been forgotten for centuries. Some never were before. Personal and cultural reinventions are as real as sunlight, ideas, and empathy. Yes is often the answer. Other answers include Breathe, Release, Gratitude, Healing, Clarity, Touching, Laughter, Connectivity, Drawing, Humor, Speaking, Rebirth, Waves, Heartbeats, Eyeballs, Wildness, Massage, Voices, Touch, Boldness, Wonder, Gestures, Music, Willingly, Tree, Waves, Silence, Courage, Words, Gratitude, Pictures, Air, Walking, Adventure, Fondness, Gardens, Silliness, Awakening, Muses,

Serendipity, Beaches, Asking, Being, Life, Sensuality, Memory, Freedom.

Who are we? Who have we become? Who do we want to be? How do we want to feel? Where do we want to go—while breath is flowing through our bodies? Lives across our land are crying out for the best impulses inside our beating hearts to return, and to help create a new beginning. How did we wind up there? How do we return to who we can become? Create your own list of what matters to you. Make it a hastily jotted down list of a few bold feelings, or take weeks and months to compose your list. Let it be a never-ending list. What's the best each of us can imagine for each other?

Making it happen day by day makes sense, since that's how a life gets lived. Following where creativity leads, and living and connecting in open and deep ways is what matters. Open up to the creative flow state, and connect with this world in a state of wonder.

Connections matter, living here in the New Now. Connect more with who you are, and who you want to become. Connect more with those around you. Because here we are. We live in a world of strained eyes continually staring down into small screens. Finally, we've seen beyond the screen and into each other's minds. We're becoming more than we dreamed possible. We're an evolved version of who we were months ago. We live in an uneasy and distracted time in history where, pre-pandemic, information overdose has disrupted our minds. We don't need more reasons not to be present. We need to learn how to unlearn, and to ask better questions. Now, many of us are deeply connected to the flowing feelings of everyone everywhere flooding our nervous systems. Yet here we are. In a New Now. It's time to connect to our deepest core. Unbury the self who we long ago shoved aside, and see life with new eyes.

In the beginning, we understood starting each day with a song in our heart was in our best interest. Waking, touching, loving, laughing, wandering, being interested in the wonder of who we happen to be every day. In the end, life happens in more varied and wonderful ways, or at least that's how it used to be. And should be again. We must become who we were meant to be. We are all responsible for creating the next culture in the United US Wakes-Up-Finally, and unleashes the possibility of it all.

How we remain loving and creative in the face of brutal senseless wars, hinged and unhinged cultural transitions, global pandemics, mass confusion, propaganda, upheavals, despair, denials, distraction, and disengagement—is the big question worth facing.

Creativity compels change. It makes what was once lived in the imagination a tangible reality. Creativity waits for no one, but works through everyone. Creativity is in our lifeblood, as it always has been. The world is waiting, and our culture is exhausted but ready to rise up and explore the inexhaustible possibilities that are waiting backstage at the opening night of the new cultural renaissance building up and forming finally around us.

Let's be grateful that we live in this constantly changing now, and do our part to transform it for the better in each waking moment we inhabit.

Manifesto #6

When the Going Gets Weird, Just Try Telling the Truth

There's a well-known quote from the late great Hunter S. Thompson, "When the going gets weird, the weird turn pro." that feels entirely applicable to the historical moment we're now living through.

For those of us with open minds (let's start there), and have environmental, planetary, and free-thinking humanistic beliefs and tendencies, things have indeed gotten weird, and so much more.

We're inside a moment in history none of us were prepared for.

A global resurgence of a toxic mix of authoritarianism, fascism, racism, women-hating, and misguided extremist fundamentalism has gripped the planet.

Deciding whether to be on the right side of history or the wrong side of history is becoming a matter of life and death.

Which side are you on? How do you want to be remembered? Are you a life-healer, or a death-dealer? Are you on the side of the reality-deniers, who stood idly by and let the entire ecosystem of our planet collapse? Or did you strive to create impactful global-shifting solutions, that would save as many lives as possible? Do you think scientifically proven life-saving vaccines contain chips that'll track you, or are you glad you'll be breathing and living through the pandemic, and be able to spend time with your loved ones for decades to come?

Our future selves already know, and we've learned in the deepest way possible that we're all one on this blue planet, floating in a cosmic ocean of darkness. On the other side of the looking glass, the future is inclusive and diverse, welcoming, and pulling us into open-minded inclusivity with intensity and joy.

But for the moment, our going has indeed gotten weird. So, what can each of us do to turn pro?

After a multi-year media barrage of gaslighting and a steady stream of propaganda was the norm, people were hungering for deeper levels of truth. We want a healthy balance of truth and freedom to be washed over our entire being—consistently and constantly.

Lies are no longer considered to be just another form of truth. Why were they ever? Misrepresentation is lying. Constantly railing against a free press is for entertainment value is un-American. Lying just to keep in practice isn't cool. Lying is a dumb choice made by willfully ignorant people. Lying is a failure of intelligence and imagination. Lies for breakfast, lunch, and dinner—leads to body bloat. Lying every day all day long is not a winning strategy.

After decades of the dumbing down of the American culture, we've reached a turning point. The signs are here, staring back at us. Get smarter everyone, or even darker and dumber times lie ahead. From the age of one to ninety-nine, begin to cherish learning and rewire your brain with everyday reading, associating with other smart people, practicing a creative pursuit of any type, and finding more things you're passionate about. Whether its writing, art, science, technology, psychology, cooking, coding, farming—you name it—dive in and become who you're meant to be in this lifetime.

Read. Write. Take a photo. Write a manifesto. Paint a picture. Recite a poem.

Write a manifesto on Love, Creativity, Interplanetary Travel, Animal Rights, Human Rights, Global Freedoms, Intuition, Empathy, Ranting, Randomness, Joyfulness, Universal Acceptance, Dreaming Bigger Dreams.

In this historical time, we've been shaken to our core, and we're feeling new awakenings. We're waking up to creating a better tomorrow today, where we'll create a smarter, more inquisitive, and more empathetic generation.

Truth is life and breath. Truth can't be shoved aside from the everyday dialogue any longer. Truth is how the weather feels on our skin. How we act as a country is created each day with every action we take.

Begin in your neighborhood, and then create the city you want to live in, that you can feel proud of for your entire lifetime. Truth is more essential now than ever before.

Words and language and written communication matter. Literacy is a superpower. People are constantly reading online, everything from the daily news reports to novels, nonfiction collections to journals, and political opinion pieces to personal essays.

The history of these vivid years and the decades ahead will be fascinating to future historians, and those of us putting down our experience at this moment in time are adding to the picture of what our world looked like.

All art, writing, music, poetry is essential art, writing, music, and poetry. We're living through a turning point in history. Document it dearly. Record it daily. Take it in completely. Tell your story. Let the future know which side you were on.

Manifesto #7 / The Internet is Always Turned On (Part 1.)

Everyone looks their best on the Internet.

Some people use the Internet for good purposes, and others use it for bad purposes.

Unless (or until) a worldwide electrical grid blackout occurs, perhaps caused by an asteroid or overactive sunspots, or just a chain reaction due to the electrical grid's servers going down, the Internet will continue to live on and connect the inhabitants of the world, for better and for worse.

The Internet is always turned on.

Everyone feels better when they're on the Internet.

The Internet always tells the truth.

The Internet usually lies about telling the truth.

There are some seriously messed-up people on the Internet.

The Internet isn't a good place to look for psychological advice.

The Internet is ravenous and must constantly be fed.

Someone just baked cupcakes (with rainbow sprinkles on them), a nice juicy steak, chocolate cream puffs, nine vegan pizzas, and a bucket of spicy shrimp. All for the Internet.

The lies the Internet tells are in direct proportion to how good your hair looks.

Don't believe anything the Internet tells you before your first cup of coffee.

The Internet wants you to spell LIFE in all caps, especially when referring to your own LIFE.

The Internet shines the light of wondrous amazing
truth to all its followers.

The Internet wants you to be wealthy and successful.

The Internet wants to know your secret inner name
that only you call yourself.

The Internet wants you to be AFRAID.

The Internet wants you to be free from all
your FEARS.

The Internet is sorry about what happened last
weekend, and it wants to make it up to you by taking
you out to dinner.

The Internet is a pagan priestess from
ancient Caledonia.

The Internet misses rave culture at its peak.

The sucky thing is the Internet is really kind at heart,
but no one understands how difficult it is being
the Internet.

The Internet is gobbling up your brain.

The Internet totally loves your new hairdo.

The worst things happen on the Internet.

The best things happen on the Internet.

Ask and you'll receive the Internet's blessings.

The Internet reports fact-based science.

Choose to believe or disbelieve in the power of the Internet. Totally up to you.

The Internet is whispering words of encouragement only you can hear.

The Internet thinks The Beats, The Beatles, and Beyoncé are cool.

The Internet wishes only the best for you in all your endeavors.

The Internet doesn't think you're taking yourself seriously enough.

The Internet believes what you believe.

The Internet thinks you're taking yourself way too seriously.

As long as we have the Internet, everything can be turned around.

The Internet is in a hateful mood lately.

People find love on the Internet. People find hate on the Internet. So, what'll be your choice today? Chill, Internet. Smoke some old school mildly buzzy super-weed, like one can legally procure in Colorado, Oregon, Illinois, California, or Washington State.

The Internet is better at giving advice than taking advice.

The Internet knows what really landed at Roswell, New Mexico in 1947, but it's not telling.

The Internet loves how day-old cold pizza tastes, right out of the fridge. Oh, also Indian and Thai food!

The Internet thinks everything has already gone to Hell in a handbasket.

The Internet thinks things are finally getting back on track.

The Internet loves the idea of a worldwide cultural renaissance.

The Internet wonders what you were thinking when you bought those shoes.

The Internet was created in the 1950s, based on the concepts of packet networking. The first computer-to-computer message was sent from a computer science center lab at the University of California (UCLA), Los Angeles.

Pursuing Happiness

A declaration of reinvention

Near the top of the Declaration of Independence are several key words that have left a lasting impact on our culture. These words state that every citizen has the right to life, liberty, and the pursuit of happiness.

Looking back to the time when this document was written, it's clear how the insertion of these words was a brilliant choice of concepts to include in this founding document, which has been studied and debated since it was composed.

We're already alive if we're capable of reading the words "life, liberty, and the pursuit of happiness," so that's a given. But wait. Life, as in the good life?

Life, as in reaching for your dreams? Life, as in continually growing and giving back to the best of your ability to the culture you live in?

Liberty is a tricky one too. Liberty to do what exactly? Here you go, have a cup of liberty, filled to the brim. No, wait, that's too much. We actually meant a thimble full. Liberty to do, be, strive for and keep figuring out what in the whole wide world one wants to do with this wondrous gift of liberty. Liberty to feel free and safe from all forms of senseless violence anywhere in your city, state, country? Liberty to be spiritual and not religious? Liberty to love freely and openly? Liberty to be open minded, and be full of liberality and loving kindness?

The third one is the most open to interpretation. The pursuit of happiness. Really? I can pursue, go on a quest for, chase after, be open to, keep on struggling to locate happiness? Thanks Declaration. Here's why this phrase has been problematic for over 200 years. Every individual defines this vague concept with wildly different interpretations. Which is part of the beauty and wonder of our culture. There's an extremely good chance your pursuit of happiness isn't going be my pursuit of happiness. Think of just a few of the variables at work here. Differences in age, socio-economic factors, race, belief-systems, emotional intelligence, political views, and sexual orientations and identifications. Go ahead. Toss a few of these variables in a blender and serve them up to the community at large. What makes every person in your household happy? How about your neighborhood? The city you live in? You won't see any agreement once you move away from one or two people you know, who you are kind of maybe sure about their likes and dislikes.

What our culture wants us to believe is that by pursuing money, wealth, and fame—we'll eventually reach happiness. Maybe this cultural construct was there from the start, and is the secret underlying message in our founding documents. To think that a room full of money equals the elusive goal of happiness is a powerful concept, but it's just as accurate as saying you'll always be happy if you live in the right neighborhood in the perfect city, meet the ideal partner, write a brilliant screenplay, live to be 100, change the world. or raise genius kids. Moments and weeks of happiness will occur at some point in all our lives. Whether it comes by chasing after it, or if it just shows up on your doorstep one afternoon with a suitcase full of daydreams and confetti is another matter altogether.

What a grand gesture. The pursuit of happiness, codified into the founding document of a newly emerging nation. The nerve of those guys. And wow, the wit and heart of them to incorporate such an idea into a founding document. Happiness as an ideal to reach for and maybe not ever attain, but these colonial founders at least wanted to plant the idea. Happiness should be pursued.

What if more than pursuing happiness had been included in the Declaration of Independence?

- How about pursuing truth?
- What about pursuing love?
- How about pursuing the fruits of the imagination and what it can create?
- When should we begin more diligently pursuing world peace?
- How about pursuing empathy and compassion?

None of the above ideas are codified in the Declaration. Instead, we were given the green light to chase after happiness—wherever it may lead. Is it time to add some more specific ideas, ones that directly relate to our times? Should we update our founding documents? Happiness is a fine aim, in a general sense, under most circumstances. Although, one person's happiness is another person's joy.

Another person's happiness is someone else's deep sense of wonder. Then again, one person's happiness can step on someone's toes. Someone's idea of happiness may be taking away your rights, which is as wrong as the day is long. Truth be told, there are many other states of being and aims people strive for over the course of their lives. Maybe it's time to filter in a wider selection of the highest qualities making up the whole of human experience.

Manifesto #8 Reinventing Making Connections

Changing the world has to be fun

> "Well I got to keep it going keep it going full steam / Too sweet to be sour too nice to be mean / On the tough guy style I'm not too keen / To try to change the world I will plot and scheme."
> – **Adam Yauch**, 1964-2012

As social creatures, we're all wired to connect to people who make us feel good.

The challenge and fun of life is in finding those who we most enjoy spending time with. We know we've found them when we laugh uncontrollably, smile easily, breathe easier, and just be ourselves.

Laughter is the original and most effective social glue. Best to experience it early, freely, and often with others. And continue to keep doing so throughout your life.

Let us resolve to joyfully change the world.

We engage in life by talking, touching, transmitting transformative ideas and emotions in real time.

Early in year one of the pandemic, millennia of physical, cultural, social hardwiring put us on pause. Humanity was asked, for its own good to stay away from groups, not be as social, and wait it out, sheltering inside. Even for naturally introverted people, those times weren't easy.

In just a few months, massive worldwide cultural shifts occurred in the blink of billions of eyes. All of this made it even more necessary to stay connected to those you care about, and to build new connections through technology.

Exchanging ideas is another thing we humans are wired to do. Prior to the pandemic, most of us had already adapted to long-distance technologically communicating.

New ideas and reinventions go hand in hand. Ideas, once formulated travel quickly by texts, video clips, and social media.

Opening a text or a video can lead to opening a mind. Globally, ideas are transmitted that feel as if they are moving at the speed of light, changing minds in the moment.

In the early twentieth century, people sat around listening to the radio—with songs and stories broadcast across the airwaves creating pictures in their minds. Now, streaming music and podcasts serve a similar purpose. Rewiring our nervous systems while reminding us of who we are in our heart of hearts, sending us songs and sounds that'll make us feel energized, change our moods, alter our physiology. Music is the art form that connects heart, mind, and spirit.

How does a particular experience make you feel inside? You don't decide, you just feel it in less than an eye blink. Art, design, media, culture have merged.

We act, or react, because we are drawn toward or pushed away from something. We're sensing the immediacy of the world at a time when it feels like the planet needs humanity to be changing a decade's worth of history in a single day.

Planetary change is speeding up, and our minds and bodies are evolving.

When ideas shared between several people connect to others and then coalesce into group knowledge, the culture shifts. Having new ideas accepted has never been easy, but it's an essential component of shifting cultures forward.

We are knowledge seekers and pattern decoders, always have been. Ingesting new ideas daily rewires your brain.

The world has altered, and a worldwide shift is in process. People are wired into global events, humanistic causes, transformative media platforms, and are ready to change the world.

The perfect ideas matter. Slightly imperfect ideas put into motion matter even more. Transformational ideas matter more than ever. Community-altering ideas are vital and necessary. Transmitting ideas at the right time leads to personal, social, cultural reinvention. Great ideas like to hang out with better ideas and improve their game. Inspiring ideas step up and let you know the time is now.

In the New Now, people have the time to think more deeply and write down what a more perfect union, life, future, would look and feel like.

Every type of relationship is a union. For a moment or a lifetime. Think about how you can make more perfect unions, knowing perfection won't be reached. But it must be reached for.

The most lasting change often arrives from inspired individuals who understand how daily actions overcome deeply embedded cultural reinforcement. Inhaling life-altering truths is essential. Exhaling toxic societal propaganda is a necessary practice, like walking and eating what makes your own body healthier. Building up a greater capacity for creation instead of destruction moves us all toward more fulfilled lives.

Interacting with people who deeply understand you feels good, and so does being around people, events, books, music, that'll alter your perceptions and open your mind.

Freethinkers will continue to build on the legacy of acceptance that permeates the global culture in this new century. People have been starving (mentally, emotionally, spiritually) for the changes already happening, and about to be.

We now rejoin the world we are creating, already in progress.

Open minds are necessary in the Age of Reinvention. People with backwards and intolerant belief systems are going to go the way of the dinosaurs, not in a hundred years, and not in two years. They are already vanishing before our eyes. Open-minded people are creating and letting culture-shifting ideas into their minds and becoming a reinvented version of themselves.

Laughing, connecting, open hearts and minds are the strongest joyful weapons we can use to shift humanity forward.

Manifesto #7 / The Internet is Always Turned On (Part 2.)

The Internet is a glorious world-changing phenomenon on the scale of the printing press.

The Internet is suddenly feeling very shy.

The Internet thinks you're fantastic. Truly.

The Internet wants you to get all the attention you so richly deserve.

The Internet loves your dark side.

The Internet encourages you to go there.

The Internet knows you can go even farther out there. So go on.

On the other hand, the Internet wants you to dial it back.

The Internet is feeling like a moody adolescent with no desire to leave their room.

The Internet is feeling like a 100-year-old who wants to party and get it on.

The Internet is inherently awesome.

As long as the Internet is around, the world will never end.

The Internet thinks you've finally gone too far.

The Internet isn't actually into cat videos, but it swoons and coos at video clips of baby pandas.

The Internet is considering getting a tattoo of your face on its upper arm.

The Internet exists in the eternal now.

The Internet has always been and always will be.

The Internet just drank seven cups of strong coffee in a row. Make that eight.

The Internet often thinks the whole world is batshit crazy.

The Internet is nostalgic for the twentieth century.

The Internet misses Bowie and Aretha and Cohen and Prince.

The Internet appreciates big mysteries and random possibilities.

The Internet is into cave paintings.

The Internet likes jazz, hip-hop, soul, and funk.
If the Internet could have anything that it can't have, it would be a massage.

After that, you could order the Internet a messy, dripping cheeseburger, with all the fixings.

The Internet believes springtime is for lovers.

The Internet wants the world to feel like it's always summertime.

The Internet is in a silly mood today and wants to skip along the sidewalk wearing a harlequin costume, singing a jolly song.

The Internet can't wait to see what's going to happen next.

Whatever the world has in store for the next few years, the Internet will have something to say about it.

The Internet has opinions.
(Which aren't necessarily facts.)

The Internet is feeling big-hearted lately, and it wants you to feel the same way.

The Internet will always fit perfectly into those black skinny jeans.

The Internet is glad that people actually read things on the Internet.

The Internet is a big proponent of literacy.

The Internet wants you to repost this.

The Internet is cautiously optimistic.

The Internet wants the inhabitants of our world to get along so much better than they're currently getting along. It wonders how the hell things grew so troubled and full of turmoil and damned difficult across the globe. Wars raging, daily shootings and senseless murders, violence baked-in from the cradle—built on layers of generational lies passed down to children who are being taught to serve nothing except hatred. The Internet doesn't see the point of faulty belief systems that encourage people to kill other people randomly. The Internet thinks NOTHING has been proven, gained, or helped by this horrid behavior.

The Internet is all for lasting peace and goodwill toward fellow humans.

We the People Declare a Worldwide Align With Reality Day

Get back on the highway leading to smarts, arts, and growing bigger hearts

Once upon a time, it was a good thing to be smart in the United States. Smart people moved our culture ahead in brilliant ways, writing culture-shifting and mind opening books, created scotch tape that worked, and building rocket ships that flew to the moon. Smart people possessed visions and dreams we still talk about today.

And now, we've endured decades of the dumbing down of the American educational system, and putting a silly notion in peoples' heads that appearing smart, brilliant, a genius, or being an expert in your field is somehow suspect or wrong. What? LP vinyl record scratch movie moment! How the Hell did we get here? And how do we get out of the Stupid Zone as quickly as possible?

Declare it's good to pick up a book, freely and often. Read whatever you want to read. Ignore the ones who want to stifle the growth of your mind, heart, and spirit. Read every day. Don't know what you want to know about? Just follow your nose. You get to decide what you want to put inside your mind.

If global pandemics can become a daily reality in the blink of an eye, so can creating a world that's better for all of us addressing the Climate Emergency now, by making a global green agenda a primary issue. We've done the impossible already. We've already been to the moon. Now, how about saving the planet for future generations? We've already created healthcare systems and vaccines in record time that have saved millions of lives. We've already been led by people with smarts and hearts. Sometimes, letting history repeat itself is a good thing. We need smart humans who want to be writers, artists, poets, political leaders (with hearts), scientists, doctors, musicians, healers, architects, world-changers, future-builders, and visionaries.

It's time to declare intelligence as one of the key elements of being human—and one of the most important tools we'll use to figure out a way to deal immediately with the next viral pandemic and the global Climate Emergency that's already here, and will continue dangerously disrupting our lives on Earth.

During the first weeks of pandemic lockdown in the United States, with no air travel overhead, and freeway congestion coming to a standstill, the sky in Los Angeles was visibly clearer. How good would it be to have cleaner air every single day in the New Now? Do we want to go back to bad air and poorer health?

Facing the reality of our situation shows intelligence. Wanting to alter our reality for the betterment of all humanity is worth striving for. Shifting our culture in ways that lift us all is a massively important goal.

When every child on the planet sees the massive scope of the problem of a Climate Emergency more clearly than many elected officials, it's time to make fundamental changes in how elected officials are held responsible—not just in this current political moment, but for future generations. Now's the time to begin asking every politician, placed both high and low, in and out of office, what can each of us do, today.

Up until a short while ago, the Climate Crisis was falsely presented as one political party against the other, when reality itself was called into question.

The dialogue has now become smart science-minded, reality-based humans against humans who are OK with destroying our home planet.

If you're a Climate Science Denier, you're clearly not in touch with your senses. It's on the news every single day. If you walk outside you'll experience it. The Climate Emergency has already ravaged our planet with superstorm-sized hurricanes and continent-engulfing wildfires. The oceans are literally rising. Every state in the United States, and every continent on the planet has been impacted by the Climate Crisis. It's only going to get more intense, dangerous, and deadly. Wildfires in Canada and the United States are worsening year by year. It's literally been unsafe to go outside and breathe in toxic air in Portland, Seattle, and New York City. If, after having witnessed these events, you're still a Climate Science

Denier, here's some good advice: step away from the smartphone that's smarter than you, and seek professional help. The obvious changes in our climate that occurred before the global pandemic brought human life on Earth to a standstill, and should've gotten your attention. Scroll through your news feed. It's there every day. Scientists have connected the dots, and have confirmed that, yes, what's going on with our first global pandemic is associated with the eco-disasters that've already swept the planet.

We're smarter than this as a culture, and as a species. Back in the 1960s and 70s, we were on the track to being smarter as a whole, back when everyone could receive a higher education without accruing a massive debt burden. Time to say no way, go back, turn around. Get back on the highway that leads to smarts, arts, and growing bigger hearts.

Smart is cool. Dumb is a decision. Libraries are free in every city. Digital and physical bookstores are wonderful to wander through. Independent bookstores are national treasures. The Strand Bookstore, in New York City; Powell's Books, in Portland, Oregon; Elliott Bay Books, in Seattle; the venerable and historic City Lights Booksellers & Publishers, in San Francisco. Any book lover who has set foot inside these temples of books has felt a sense of awe and gratitude for the written word. Never in the history of our species inhabiting this globe has such an impossibly overwhelming number of books been at anyone's fingertips. You can read yourself silly or mad, read until your mind is aglow, and read for comfort, joy, self-knowledge, and clarity.

In the middle of the twentieth century, cultural intellectuals representing every point of view were on major talk shows, tossing around big brain ideas, and discussing culturally diverse thoughts and doing so with informed opinions. Seeing brilliant writers and public intellectuals on TV programs, often in a format where they could talk at length, and transform the social dialogue with conversations lasting for half an hour was an education on how language and thought could meld seamlessly together and entertain, as well as intelligently comment on the world.

For those who can sense it, there's something in the air again—possibilities are expanding, along with the intelligence and empathy of curious people. Humans are finding out they're capable of being much more than they ever believed possible. People are living longer, evolving quicker. Same is true for the upcoming generations. Only more so.

Children have taken over the Climate Emergency conversation, and this is thrilling to behold. It's the direction the world is going—smarter, more assertive children speaking up and saving the planet. One has to applaud them and marvel at the stark difference from how things used to be. People who want to turn the clock backwards are consumed by fear. Today's children are fearlessly full of wonder.

Even if you look the other way, the rest of us are doing what it takes to create a greener and more sustainable world. Honor your own experiential truth, and step aside from the constant churn of the brainwashing media machinery. Don't kid yourself. The Climate Crisis isn't a debate. We've already crossed that threshold. It's happening and intensifying. People in the desert are experiencing wildfires. In the desert.

Every country in the world must dedicate themselves to pursuing a green agenda, and move past the senseless wars and cultural and behavioral norms that could eventually destroy humanity.

Globally, cultures must shift to a human rights perspective. There's already been enough senseless brutality inflicted upon women and children due to outmoded culturally reinforced rules of conduct installed thousands of years ago. Uninstall these foolish codes of conduct destroying the lives of girls and women.

It's time to shift our focus. Turn dreamers into doers, and planners into makers. We can create a future world where war is replaced by acts of loving kindness. After the recent worldwide waves of divisive wrongheaded backwards-looking populist movements, it's time for the opposite. It's time to create the New Now we've all collectively dreamed about for centuries.

With these things in mind, let's declare that intelligence, creativity, and loving kindness go hand in hand, and are the guiding lights in a free and open society. Declare that Climate Emergency Deniers shouldn't be allowed to even pretend to be political leaders. Declare an end to dumb being cute or anywhere near acceptable. Declare we can all aim to become kinder, more empathetic, and yes, even more curious, and wonder-filled today than yesterday.

Manifesto #9 / Now is the Time to Think about Reinventing Our Future

Create a Department of The Future: Communication, compassion, and future visions

Kids are stepping up and behaving like the adults in the room. They've taken it upon themselves to address the critical nature of changing our behavior around the accelerating Climate Crisis. They understand how it's now up to them to get the word out every day, and begin remaking the world we live in. Probably not the burden they were expecting to be hoisted on their shoulders, but that's the cards they've been dealt.

We aren't living in a time when incremental change will do. We're living in an age when big ideas about making things better aren't just important, but vital. The Climate Crisis is happening now. All you have to do is walk outside to know this truth.

But, even the concept of truth has been chipped away at, through years of propaganda broadcast on TV and the Internet. TV asks, "Who you gonna believe, me, or your own lying eyes?" TV was our friend when all it talked us into was buying candy and soda we didn't need, but now it's brainwashing us with thoughts we don't need.

We need a Department of The Future in the White House, to make daily assessments on the progress made in addressing the ongoing Climate Emergency, reality-based conversations on how to create global peace initiatives, transparent talks on how to immediately address the global inequality of women and children, and actionable policies to take meaningful steps about daily human rights violations, also mostly directed at women and children anywhere and everywhere in the world. You can probably think up several more on your own.

Historians like to point out that democracy in America is a messy process. It's set up to be slow and cumbersome, but common sense and our gut intuition tells us this approach stopped working long before the pandemic. No, not common sense in a "the whole governmental system's broken kind of way, and we must privatize Social Security madness" but in a "let's actually bring back common sense" type of way. Immediate solutions are required. About the Climate Emergency, Democracy, and worldwide Human Rights. Sometimes it seems like a single decision-maker would be far more efficient. But everyone knows those types of leaders are called Kings and Queens (or these days, Dictators), and our Founders sailed on leaky wooden boats across a vast ocean to escape a mad king and those types of humanity-stifling social structures.

While our original Founding documents have held up as sturdy social and legal tools over the past few centuries, perhaps we need a Declaration of Interdependence, as well as a Declaration of Independence. If, at this moment, we don't truly understand we're all in this together, one has to wonder what it will take. It's been made as clear as a hurricane force wind slamming you to the ground, how the fundamental necessity of implementing transformative social change is now a matter of survival. Meaning, of course, social transformations that benefit all. As in Liberty and Justice for All.

Why not begin at the source? Start by forming a new governmental department: The Department of The Future. While we're at it, create the Department of Human Rights. We're all human beings. This should be important enough for us all to get behind. There are enough brilliant minds in our country to establish such departments and make them a reality. Time to lay the groundwork for a kinder society that takes care of everyone's health concerns without bankrupting people is a good place to begin. If the United States doesn't create and follow through on these types of global initiatives, who will? Canada and Sweden are prime examples of socially effective healthcare systems proven to work. Simply brushing off these workable systems as too costly or too socialist isn't a real, much less thoughtful answer.

Our culture is starving for new and impactful solutions that aren't part of a ten-year plan, but will deliver results this year, this month. People need help now. A culture where people aren't pushed out of the system and left to fend for themselves is a good culture to imagine, and a necessary one to build. Envisioning a society where improving education isn't fought over or debated in code—but reinvented by people with open minds used on a continual basis, is a culture-shifting idea most intelligent people can agree upon.

History has finally pushed us ahead, as a species and a culture. We're still experiencing a full-on shock to the system, still dealing with the aftereffects of the worldwide pause, and a complete reassessment of how we live our lives. The reinvention of social, cultural, and political dialogue is already underway.

Intelligent and spirited young people, across the globe, have shown us the way, shifting the cultural paradigm around whether children could lead us or not. Turns out they can, and they are. They deserve our deep respect for what they've started. They've led, and inspired, older generations who have been lifelong activists.

It's time to begin creating a future built on smarter ideas, real cooperation and compassion, and using the ongoing cultural reinvention we used to be known for around the world. These future visions will take us deeper into the New Now.

Manifesto #7 / The Internet is always Turned On (Part 3.)

The Internet is determined to stay cautiously optimistic, no matter what.

The Internet wants some fresh and tasty sushi. Right now!

The Internet would like some top shelf sake to go with that sushi order.

When spring finally arrives, the Internet will be marching in the streets.

When the Internet comes marching in, the whole city will be filled with joy.

When the Internet strolls down the street in its finery, you'll smile and shake your head in wonder.

The Internet wants to help everyone, and it thinks everyone is essentially good at heart.

The Internet is completely into the idea of humans living on other planets, but it wants our home planet revived to optimum shape first.

The Internet is becoming a living,
breathing organism.

The Internet is alive inside your mind.

The Internet is as calm as a cucumber.

The Internet wants you to calm down too.

The Internet is talking a mile a minute about something you don't really want to know about.

The Internet says what it really thinks.

The Internet yells out loud in joy or frustration.

The Internet isn't a big fan of Climate Science Deniers. I mean come on, experiential evidence anyone? Where do you live? Has the weather there gotten beyond extreme? Far beyond unpredictable? Dangerous daily? Exactly!

The Internet doesn't suffer fools gladly.

The Internet speaks daily with the Golden Goddess Creative Flow Energy Gaia Loving Kindness Cosmic Network.

The Internet is single and ready to mingle.

The Internet just drank a whole bottle of the best red wine it could find online.

The Internet is full of vitality and visions.

The Internet thinks we have to take a stand for things we believe in.

The Internet is starting to get really pissed off.

The Internet isn't messing around today.

The Internet wakes up early, stays up late, and gets down to business in between.

The Internet has just changed its mind. Cat videos are super deluxe cool.

The Internet is in love with love.

The Internet love love loves how you look in that outfit.

The Internet asks for your forgiveness.

Yes, people do find love, kindness, and caring humans on the Internet. This makes the Internet feel warm and fuzzy.

The Internet is Spiritual but not Religious.

The Internet has looked ahead several centuries, and it assures us we're going to make it.

The Internet is into Werner Herzog, but seriously, who isn't?

The Internet knows the difference between lying, stretching the truth, telling a whopper, eating a Whopper, fabricating, eliminating the truth from your whole being, being a lying sack-o-crap, lying to stay in practice, lying as a lifestyle, ready to lie at a moment's notice, lying for no bloody good reason at all, lying for the gosh-durned fun of it all, being a deceitful blowhard, lying as a game, taking it lying down, lying as a way to attempt to game the system, and lying to protect bigger lies that are hiding behind gold-plated locked doors.

Culture Is Not a Luxury

Art can change lives and save lives.

In the New Now, in this historical moment, when nature has pushed the reset button on humanity, we gain comfort and joy from movies, books, music, TV shows, poetry, in every conceivable form.

The arts entertain us, calm us, enliven us, and touch the core of our being.

This has been true over the course of human history, and it's especially true now.

All the artifacts, sculptures, architecture, paintings, poetry, plays, and music handed down to us through the centuries have told us what our global ancestors felt and thought about the world they observed. The history of humanity is known and understood only by the arts and artifacts left behind.

Art and Culture, Liberal Arts, Dramatic and Performing Arts—are studied in school at every level. The students who study these subjects have a higher degree of emotional intelligence. They were drawn toward the arts since the arts spoke to them, often at a young age. While the value of art and culture is reinforced by our most popular art forms of TV shows, music, and movies, how we each consider the role of art in our lives comes back to how they make us feel.

Do you love art? Of course you do. If a movie ever made you lose track of time and you became emotionally invested in the characters' lives, you know the importance of art. If a song fills you with joy or makes you weep, you were touched by the arts.

Art and Culture is what gets us through good times and bad. We seek out movies and music to remind us we aren't alone, we are understood, and we're part of collective humanity.

We want to share enjoyable experiences with the people we most want to be with.

Whether people relate storytelling on a TV show or the hit songs on Billboard's Hot 100 to every form of art and culture through the ages doesn't matter. What matters is that artists are still creating paintings, photographers are taking pictures, moviemakers are making movies, writers are writing novels, and songwriters are writing songs.

We see our lives and our perspective on life reflected back through our culture. In the United States, these culture-shifting moments include Lee Krasner working on a mural for the WPA arts program in the 1930s, Jackson Pollack dripping paint on a canvas in his Long Island studio in the 1950s, Robert Rauschenberg creating his Combines in the late 1950s and early 1960s in lower Manhattan, and Dustin Yellin encasing thousands of tiny images in polymer to create mini-monolithic digital-age collages in the 2010s. All these visual art creators represent the world they found themselves in, and made sense of it in their own way. And they each proved one thing: Art is a necessity for our culture and the world.

All art is interrelated. As are all artists. Musicians are called Artists. Actors are called Artists. Painters are called Artists. We call on Artists to take us out of ourselves, and bring us deeper into ourselves. It's a massively wonderful mission, and every artist is up to it.

How many countless hours of inspiration which led to culture-shifting ideas and inventions came from watching a movie, listening to music, or viewing a work of art in a museum or a book? In the same way a doctor spends countless hours learning to be a doctor, an artist learns by countless hours of learning from creations from the past, and applying this knowledge to the cultural now. After learning what's been done and mixing it with what's inside of them, they get to bend the rules and create with total freedom in their chosen art form. Otherwise, what's the fun?

Deciding whether a child should learn to be an artist or a doctor isn't an either or decision. Every society must have both. Could we live without music or movies during this time period?

Art gives people ideas enabling them to grow past boundaries. Art is the dreamworld present in real-time and the reason why we can imagine a better world. Art breaks through online algorithms and changes the course of history.

Art touches every part of our lives and shapes us from the time we're small children. Art provides much needed emotional intelligence, beauty, and thoughtfulness in a world driven mad by over-objectivity and precision for the sake of precision. To think the world can get along without creative aspirations and new creations in every form possible is to imagine a bland, uninteresting world no one should be forced to even think about, much less live in.

A Declaration of Interdependence #2

We the People declare it's a brand-new day—with a heart-centered way of communicating.

We the People are walking down the center of car-less streets, making our own path in the New Now.

We the People declare love is still the word. And always will be.

We the People are becoming who we were always meant to become in this lifetime.

We the People declare freedom of the press is needed now more than ever, and it's an essential and fundamental right.

We the People declare we're waking up in a new morning, a new day, a new place in time.

We the People declare we deserve leaders with heart, intelligence, and a vision for the future that aligns with reality. This isn't too much to ask for, as massive wildfires, half-century droughts, and superstorm hurricanes and bomb cyclones have already ravaged the planet.

We the People declare open-hearted humans with their finger on the pulse of basic human needs are needed now.

We the People are standing on fire escapes in Hell's Kitchen, feeling cool nighttime air on our skin, and banging on pots and pans.

We the People declare that science never was and never will be a dirty word. Same for: democratic, liberal, expert, free press, socialism, intelligence, progressive, creativity, free will, and humanism.

We the People are putting our shoulder to the wheel of change, and pushing the culture forward.

We the People declare loving kindness is hardwired into our DNA.

We the People celebrate Healers, Leaders, Musicians, Scientists, Artists, Chefs, Athletes, Writers, Shamans, Dancers, Protectors, Builders, Architects, Poets, Philosophers, Photographers, Visionaries, and Intuitives.

We the People declare we are speaking up, holding onto each other, and upleveling our culture.

We the People are feeling the healing of the planet, and never want to move backwards again. No more dirty-colored skies, factory-farmed foods, congested streets, or treating the Earth horribly. No more being led down wrong roads to nowhere, and no more inequality on any level of society.

We the People are stronger than before and are truly feeling the weight and the lightness within us.

We the People declare we are here at this moment in history for a reason. We're the ones who were meant to cut through mass confusion, and to implement immediate cultural shifts based on clarity and empathy.

We the People made it through to the other side, and celebrate those who came through with us.

We the People are sending out a greater sense of peace all across the planet, from every caring heart.

We the People are the people we've been dreaming about for centuries. And we've finally woken up.

We the People know we'll eventually feel lighter in our hearts, and that's when the real work will begin.

Lower the Voting Age to 16, and several more commonsense solutions

Since the global pandemic has rolled across our land, causing death, sickness, and loss of every kind— voting by mail which many states have been doing for decades, has been a commonsense way to go.

It was understood that people want more choices in how they vote, and not fewer.

What's become clear, is that younger citizens in the United States must be allowed to vote to protect their lives and their future.

The time has come. More voters lead to a stronger democracy. What if there were a way to add millions of newer, younger voters?

How about voting by smartphone and email?

Voting by mobile phone would bring out more young voters, without a doubt.

Voting by mobile phone will change the voting demographic in a single election, two at the most.

Massive smartphone turnout for the 2028 presidential election, anyone?

Along with making it easier (not continually adding more barriers to casting a ballot) to vote, let's consider lowering the voting age to 16.

During the Vietnam war era, the argument was made that if one could fight and die for our country, one should have the right to vote at the age of 18. And so, the voting age was lowered.

Now, we're living in a time of a mass shooting epidemic, a lingering global pandemic, and a Climate Crisis that's just ramping up. If kids in school are expected to learn in a classroom that could be turned into a war zone at any moment, the same rules for voting must apply. If children are expected to put their lives on the line to get an in-person education, give them the right to vote. Any United States citizen, starting at age 16 should be able to vote, especially on the gun control issue that impacts their very lives, every single day.

Vote for your life, breathable air, and a sustainable future.

It's already happened in Scotland, and is being considered in Canada.

In 2015, Scotland lowered the voting age to 16, to vote in Scottish Parliamentary and local council elections. In 2020, Canadian Senator Marilou McPhedran brought forth a bill to lower the voting age from 18 to 16, for federal elections.

To all of the brainy tech wizards living in the United States willing and able to change history for the better (according to reality, not delusions): Get to work making it safe and secure to vote mobile in upcoming presidential elections.

Start creating, developing, and building an app that can be street legal for the November 2028 election. Mobile-ready, safe, un-hackable by subversive groups and disruptive individuals or groups in our country, and/or Russian hackers. There's your creative brief. Have at it.

Voting by smartphone is the ideal safe voting solution geared for this moment in history, and not just another reason for politicians to let down the American people. Everyone carries around a phone connected to the Internet. Voting via Internet is already being done, by United States citizen living overseas.

Political leaders, you too can step up and make a stand for democracy it. Turn this into your issue—think about voting by mail and smartphone as a lifesaving tool, to make society ready—before the next pandemic, electrical grid attack, or power-disrupting superstorm rolls into town.

Along with the technology and security connected with voting, there must be a complete shift in thinking about the eligible age for voting.

Since younger people have already stepped up and shown they possess the courage and knowledge to add to the global conversation by coming up with workable solutions to the Climate Crisis, they deserve to choose the next leaders of our country. They should be the ones who are deciding their future. The right to vote should be lowered to 16, Before we vote for president of the United States in November 2028.

By lowering the voting age to 16, a greater number of young people will have a voice in the political conversation, and completely change our political system for generations to come. Naturally, the pure outrage of youth will help to end voter suppression, gerrymandering, corporate billions buying politicians by the cartload, and speaking out against every other form of corrupt voting practice.

When Franklin Delano Roosevelt signed the Social Security Act in 1935, he was creating a financial and cultural safety net for that time and for future generations. We've all met someone who has benefitted from this plan, and it's time for visionary political leaders to step forward to protect for the future, and expand this vital national governmental benefit. If one party can install far-right extremists to sit on the Supreme Court, and broadcast that they'd be willing to take away America's Social Security benefits—informed young citizens should be there to cast a vote on this issue, for their parents and grandparents.

As in the time of FDR we need more political leaders to act, before corrupting corporate greed chips away more pieces of our democracy.

If this historical moment isn't the time for another massive cultural, social, and political shift, then what will it take? This is America's next New Deal Moment. Lives are at stake, the same way they were back in the 1930s and 40s. The citizens of the United States have seen too many rights taken away. This is wrong as wrong can be. Their eyes are open, and they've shown what smart, engaged voters who want to help create a better society look like.

It's time to welcome younger voters into the system, so they can begin changing history.

Manifesto #7 / The Internet is always Turned On (Part 4.)

The Internet wants you to choose equality, freedom, liberty, and kindness.

The Internet is the best artist in town, and it paints on walls, light poles, clouds, scraps of paper, wood, wild notions, backrooms in bars, the full moon, T-shirts, parked cars with no wheels, and subway platforms.

The Internet knows the difference between being a character and having character.

The Internet is feeling it today. Totally feeling it.

The Internet likes comedians who work blue.

The Internet knows more than it's telling.

Sometimes the Internet is overwhelmed by the willful stupidity of human beings. (Not naming any names.)

Mobility-wise, the Internet thinks expansion without transportation is strangulation.

The Internet wants to fill your heart with wonder.

The Internet is exasperated.

The Internet hates hate speech.

The Internet digs compassion and empathy.

The Internet wants you to repeat out loud: love love love love love love caring creativity breath heart love love love love love every day for a month, for starters.

The Internet is going to Barcelona on vacation. Mmmm, tapas bars, Gaudi's architecture, and Picasso's artwork.

The Internet wants to have a quick chat about your ability to rewire your brain. Did you know your brain can be rewired, as the science of neuroplasticity has shown?

The Internet thinks historical context is important, but some things are timelessly wrong. Things like committing murder, molesting or beating children, and torturing and killing animals.

The Internet believes in women having complete control of their reproductive rights.

The Internet implores you to upgrade your beliefs, since you don't seem to be living by them anyway.

The Internet knows peace, love, and goodness dwells in most of humanity's heart.

The Internet has taken over the whole Universe, and it is moving on to the Universe next door. It's going to let its sister run things for a while.

The Internet is pure love.

Reinventing How We Vote for the Next President

Think about it as one way to save democracy

It'll be coming around soon: The Presidential election season in the Divided States of America. The months are going to fly by.

Lately, every election is the most important election we've ever voted in. True to form, the 2024 presidential election is the most important election any of us will ever vote in. Horrific and murderous violence against black people, Asians, children, is at an all-time high. When you toss in women's healthcare rights stolen from them by the tainted Supreme Court, all the sanctioned and unsanctioned tricks like gerrymandering, voter suppression, and of course, the Electoral College which removes the notion of one person equals one vote. It's a lot. Stir in the big money that's damaged our political system— and it's a recipe for the most divisive and dangerous election in the history of the United States.

So, no pressure.

Along with everything else, the Climate Emergency has to be taken seriously by whomever becomes president. With the 2024 election, we'd like to propose a major change happens to the election process. Well, two things. Change the voting option to voting by mobile phone, and lower the voting age to 16-years-old. Too soon? OK, let's work on these two essential changes to voting laws across the United States by the 2028 presidential election.

Regardless, here we are. And rain or shine, it happens—every four years, less than half the country decides who's going to become the new president, or join in with the crazy mobs who want to slow down all government operations to make a political point, and screw up the functioning of democracy, again.

No matter what, a new way of structuring voting must happen. Society has drastically changed. How we vote, and at what age we can vote must be updated to reflect our current world. It's time for voting by mobile phone, and email. It's an idea whose time has arrived.

Why not make voting as easy as texting? Just go online with your phone and choose your candidate, like you choose groceries or a pair of shoes. Yes, that's what I want to buy. (Bonus: irony is built into the app.) Using our digital devices to vote is just common sense mixed with everyday convenience. Would more citizens vote if they could vote from their mobile phones? Without a doubt.

It's time to move past the days of standing in line to vote (since even that's become a divisive issue), especially when it's become a matter of life and death.

One of the things that still works about America is its ceaseless potential to reinvent itself. The workplace has been reinvented before our eyes. Working from home is one wave of the future that's already happened, and been rewired into millions of nervous systems. Too late for it to become un-rewired.

Surely we can reinvent the process of voting for a President.

So, yes. Citizens should be able to vote by mobile phone. For their own health and the health of our democracy. We already possess the technological and voter safety measures necessary. If not our mobile phones, then email is a tried and proven possibility. Overseas citizens vote by email. How about the rest of us? Isn't it time to upgrade our voting system, nationwide?

Imagine being a part of the first Vote by Phone generation. History in the making on steroids. By the time the next presidential election rolls around, we'll have already begun the process of changing the voting age to 16-years-old.

Put up billboards, send text alerts, and transmit a blaring wake-up noise to every radio and TV on election day. Just like the Emergency Alert System used to do when alerting citizens of nuclear weapons aimed at their backyard. Your phone will ring out with an early morning wake-up alert. "What's that for, Nuclear Armageddon?" "Nah, make a pot of coffee and fry up some eggs. Oh, and hand me my fully charged phone. I'm going to vote for the president and buy groceries at the same time."

History has pushed us, and we're going to propose more rights, not less. Stand up for expanding the rights we have, not have more of them stolen under the cover of night. Let's get on with it, and reinvent a fundamental part of the political system. What do we have to lose but our belief in fully functioning democracy?

Manifesto #7 / The Internet is always Turned On (Part 5.)

The Internet wants you to rethink your priorities.

The Internet is a cat whisperer.

The Internet isn't going to cry at romantic comedies anymore.

The Internet thinks tearing children from their parents at borders is a crime.

The Internet knows the difference between a Climate Crisis and winter weather. Wow, look, it's snowing!

The Internet is OCD, and loves FDR, MLK, NPR, and the BBC.

The Internet is choosing to ignore people who spout complete nonsense.

The Internet believes some of what you believe, but wow, certainly not all of it.

The Internet believes in your body's own powerful healing energy.

The Internet knows you feel better when you show up and speak up.

The Internet thinks clutter enhances creativity. No matter what anyone else says.

The Internet is thinking quantumly.

Wherever you go, the Internet is with you.

The Internet knows how to have a good time.

The Internet thinks freedom of expression is essential for all humanity.

The Internet imagines it, and then makes it happen.

The Internet is all for speaking up, and knows it's often the bravest act one ever does. In some parts of the world it's not permitted and leads to a person being murdered by their own government.

The Internet knows everyone has a voice, and some voices are silenced too soon.

The Internet sees how much you've evolved and grown over the past few years.

The Internet is moved by the millions of children and young people speaking up in the New Now. It's their future!

The Internet has had a lot on its mind lately.

The Internet is vigilant about the truth.

The Internet is about being and becoming.

The Internet remembers when trolls used to live under bridges.

The Internet doesn't endorse any product or service for sale on the Internet.

A Declaration of Interdependence #3

We the People deserve a social system and culture that is designed to benefit everyone.

We the People are caffeinated and illuminated.

We the People believe in ourselves as a force for essential change—knowing we're stronger and more resilient than ever.

We the People see limitless possibilities ahead.

We the People demand truth and transparency from every world leader, from this day forward.

We the People are now proceeding to fully reinvent the world, in a sustainable, eco-friendly way.

We the People know how interconnected we are on the planet, and we wouldn't have it any other way.

We the People finally see our planet with the clarity and consideration it deserves.

We the People are taking care of each other, our thoughts, our hearts, our present moment, and our future.

We the People believe We the People may finally mean what it's supposed to mean.

We the People are writing it down and making things happen. Everything now begins anew.

We the People are thrilled to see the planetary changes that've happened from less driving, less flying, and so much less industrial pollution. Shall we continue on this path of a sustainable future, already underway?

We the People are journaling, meditating, stretching, and making ourselves whole again.

We the People are finding new ways to be more socially culturally universally aware every day.

We the People are at the beginning of an adventure, the start of a journey, and on the cusp of a new chapter of the human history.

We the People are makers, doers, creators, re-inventors, storytellers, collectors, cooks, engineers, sculptors, connectors, scientists, communicators, empaths, philosophers, world-makers, discoverers, lovers, future-builders, instigators, abstract painters, urban mystics, teachers, peaceful warriors, wilderness wanderers, songwriters, hand-holders, and big dreamers.

We the People are feeling so much at this time and want to hug so many people, but sometimes a tree will have to do. We're all tree-huggers now.

We the People will be gentler with everyone on the planet, and treat them with more loving care.

We the People are listening to the Earth, as it tells us it wants to be healed.

We the People understand how we must build a more peaceful and sustainable world. During this time doesn't war seem horrific and insane, begun by insane people for insane false reasons?

We the People love the courage of the healers, protectors, transporters, and know they've helped us arrive here at the New Now.

We the People are in the process of shifting every social, cultural, and organizational paradigm.

We the People are undoing societal brainwashing, and installing updated mental software.

We the People are becoming exactly who we imagined we'd become.

We the People are painting walls and walking up the sides of mountains. We are talking to ducks and crows. We're seeing and feeling our own expanding future as clearly as we see this historic timeless moment.

We the People know healing hearts and minds takes time.

We the People agree it's become critical to better align with and respect nature.

We the People are telling our stories, beginning anew, embracing sunshine and storms, starting to laugh more, sitting in city parks and writing in notebooks, asking a lot of questions, and listening in a deeper way.

We the People are grateful for deep dark forests, shadow-filled mountain trails, and days just like today.

We the People are urban wanderers, mobile-texters, quantum mind achievers, wide-open space breathers, digital natives, futuristic pioneers, questioning wonderers, curious askers, right-brain creators, delirious dancers, and impactful transformers. We the People know past civilizations have faced massive natural historical planet-transforming cultural shifts, and went through some of these same things we're going through, and came out the other side.

We the People are turning the music up loud, and laughing and singing on the night the world decides it's time to come back together, and we'll help to throw the biggest celebration in the world once we're over the shock of hearing the word "YES" said over and over, and reverberating throughout the land. But we know more than ever before, patience is not a virtue. It's a skill.

We the People are elevating, questioning, expanding, and evolving.

We the People are listening to our hearts, in ways we never could before. Something's shifted.

We the People are performing good works that'll echo through time, and be spoken of by our ancestors.

We the People love the sound of seagulls as they wheel on wings over the waves.

We the People are shouting it from the rooftops: What makes us human is kindness and compassion, most of all.

We the People are viewing everything as if seeing this world for the very first time.

We the People are wondering why no one pressed the reset button on the whole planet before now.

We the People are good with loving more and transforming the entire world's culture. But wow, if we forget how to be caring and curious and silly, what was the point of all this?

Manifesto #7 / The Internet is always Turned On (Part 6.)

Once upon a time… the Internet didn't exist. (Imagine that.)

The Internet is a good egg.

It's comforting just knowing the Internet is always there for you.

The Internet is wholeheartedly against racism and sexism and ageism. We are all one, and the time has come to feel this in our hearts and bones.

The Internet loved when movie theaters were so much bigger, and not the size of shoe boxes. They were called movie palaces for a reason. You can look it up on the Internet.

The Internet knows there'll never be another voice like Aretha's voice.

The Internet wants a moratorium on stupid, vile, anti-social behavior.

The Internet gives you permission not to believe the same old lies anymore (if you ever did).

The Internet digs Bullet Trains and wonders why high-speed rail hasn't been constructed in all corners of America.

The Internet is supremely proud to have been imagined in the same century Miles Davis lived in, and created Kind of Blue.

The Internet loves egg salad sandwiches with celery and relish, and a ton of pepper.

The Internet is here to help you become the person you've always wanted to be.

The Internet misses George Carlin. Seven dirty words…brilliant.

The Internet does own a crystal ball, and it can predict the future. But it's not telling. You wouldn't believe it anyway.

The Internet is a multifaceted projection of life on another planet, living inside the stomach of an alien being.

The Internet isn't going anywhere.

The Internet wants the US Government to implement a modern version of the WPA program. Put artists to work making art and pay them a livable wage. Make society joyful. Artists shift the culture in so many ways. Songs! Paintings! Books! Poems! Plays! Dig in and feast on Arts & Culture!

Believe it or, the Internet wants you to read more books.

The Internet wants every little child in the world to be as smart as humanly possible.

The Internet believes in you.

Manifesto #10

Living in the New Now

As Yogi Berra said, "The future's not what it used to be."

In the New Now, we are creating history daily.

The New Now is really one long day going on forever.

In the New Now, it's become crystal clear the personal is universal.

Whatever else it's telling you, the New Now is saying this: It's never too late to be guided by your heart.

Whoever you were before the New Now occurred, you're going to always be a slightly better version of yourself if you travel through the New Now learning open-hearted lessons from nature.

In the New Now, history is watching, history is watching, history is watching.

The New Now is telling stories to the future, written on the night winds and whispered by shooting stars.

The New Now wants you to plant trees, hold hands, eat more vegetables.

The New Now lives in a log cabin in the deep dark woods, sits at a wooden table, and draws circles on a drawing pad all day long.

The New Now suggests getting a massage, standing in a field of wildflowers, being in the flow state.

In the New Now, it's time for every government in the world to provide its citizens with a Universal Basic Income.

The New Now is both a wake-up call, and a sleeping pill.

The New Now no longer asks how, but just knows and believes.

In the New Now, a global movement promoting equality, justice, and love has sprung up—all around the world.

The New Now suggests wandering somewhere new every day, watching black and white movies from the 1940s, painting a masterpiece on a wall in your basement.

The New Now was predicted by philanthropists, seers, scientists, and sci-fi writers. Maybe they should've spoken much louder and written everything in ALL CAPS.

The New Now has indeed sparked the Green Goddess flowing energy that's encircling the planet.

The New Now is a magic TV, a roller-skating octopus, and a free ticket to a long walk.

The New Now believes you can change the world. Oh, look, you already did!

In the New Now, the Universe is more turned on, slightly brighter, with a sharpened clarity.

The New Now is about being in the moment, transforming, remembering, dreaming, planning, rebuilding, releasing, transitioning, renewing, and reinvigorating.

In the New Now, time stops and starts up again at random intervals.

The New Now suggests words, feelings, actions.

The New Now is about being a bookworm, a knowledge-seeker, an autodidact, an eBook reader, an audible book listener, a recipe reader, a physical book reader, a daily reader, a reader of signs walls notes letters blogs, a screen reader, a cereal box reader, a wide-awake reader, a late-night digital device reader, a reader of history, a compulsive reader, a daydreaming reader, a reader of Google searches, a reader of books from the past, present, and future.

The New Now is an invisible river in the sky, of free-flowing ideas, waiting to be embraced by you on your best day.

The New Now has reset the meaning of time, our connection to nature, and our journey through each day.

The New Now is sitting in a far corner of the park,
leaning against a Pine tree, reading Leaves of Grass.

The New Now suggests writing a screenplay, walking
from wherever you are to Canada, switching from
green tea to mushroom coffee.

In the New Now, we're all responsible for creating a
new society.

We're all deeper inside ourselves in the New Now,
sometimes lost in a haze of free floating memories,
or inhabiting a place within where we're constantly
discovering unexpected new thoughts and
old remembrances.

The New Now asks more questions than it answers.
In the New Now, violent, murderous racism has
no place.

Our ears hear differently in the New Now. Voices and
music fill our minds in a more complete way.

The New Now suggests going on silent beach walks,
shaving your head, listening to the heartbeat of
your beloved.

The New Now is glad to meet you, and will send uplifting messages to your heart from time to time.

Here in the New Now, the spirit of the Earth is pushing up through the roots, grass, soil—and entering our being in ways not felt for centuries.

The New Now is offering you a chance or two to begin again. Take them.

The New Now is sitting on top of the roof, with an amazing summer day view of Puget Sound, reading the poetry of Amiri Baraka, Sonia Sanchez, and Langston Hughes.

Many experiences in the New Now are uplifting, hand-picked by ourselves or serendipity.

In the New Now, we may realize we've been brainwashed years ago, by some that meant well and others with definite ill-intent. Now, we've reached the exact wonder-filled moment when we can uninstall the previous brainwashing software, and install the reprogramming of our own choosing.

The New Now also includes long walks where you'll see bunnies in the woods, mossy rocks in streams, crows involved in intense conversations.

On some days, the New Now is sprinkling luck and miracles on the sunny sidewalk, right in front of you.

The New Now suggests writing a letter to yourself, cooking up a stir fry, drawing with your eyes closed.

The New Now is sitting on a tree stump behind the barn, swaying to Bowie's voice coming through a portable radio.

If there ever was an ideal time to build a time machine, it's at this moment in the New Now. Maybe even a big, multi-user time machine that could fit in a hundred people at a time. Wow, you could sell tickets to that thing and there would be a line stretching all the way from Miami to Los Angeles.

The New Now suggests meditation, reading food labels, asking questions, talking on the phone, cutting your own hair, journaling, laughing, and daydreaming.

The New Now is a windstorm, a symphony, a tsunami, a realignment, an infusion of kindness.

The New Now asks you to cultivate empathy daily. New ways of seeing and being resulting from the

New Now will happen all at once, and over years
and decades.

In the New Now, listen to what your inner voice tells
you, and follow it.

The New Now says it's time to make lists, take
photos, jump up and down, rest, rebuild, create,
dream bigger dreams, plan, imagine.

In the New Now, grasses, flowers, and weeds grow
wild in city parks.

The New Now is against all lies, falsehoods, untruths,
and misdirections.

The New Now wants you to add wonder and wander
to your to-do list.

Wherever we go from here, we'll carry a deeper sense
of self by going further into the New Now.

In the New Now, life shouldn't return to normal,
it should become amazingly better than what was
accepted as normal for far too long.

The New Now suggests cutting up magazines, finding
lost socks, rearranging cupboards.

We've been ready for the New Now for quite some time, and we all deserve to live in a world full of more love, kindness, laughter, empathy, compassion, and peace.

In the New Now, we'll accept and honor one another's strengths and visions.

The New Now suggests planting gardens, dancing with glee, communicating joyfully, and feeling the new world growing within yourself.

The New Now sees clearer, asks directly, arrived when it was supposed to, is ready for what's next, wants radical transformation to get underway.

In the New Now, taking care of yourself is often the best thing you can do. Luckily, this can be anything you want it to be.

The New Now suggests deep breaths, cooking with garlic and spices, being in the moment.

The New Now is texting you from prehistory, with the message written in all caps: GET IT RIGHT THIS TIME, ONLY MUCH SOONER!

Manifesto #7 / The Internet is always Turned On (Part 7.)

The Internet has already changed the way your brain works.

The Internet believes serial lying is a form of stupidity.

The Internet thinks Eric Idle should be King of the World.

The Internet is willing to change reality for your benefit.

The Internet digs two-part harmonies.

The Internet isn't going to put up with this crap
any longer.

The Internet has had enough of your kooky ideas.

The Internet is in love with every single kooky idea
in your wacky little brain.

The Internet wants you to act completely silly for an
entire day. Half a day just won't do.

The Internet knows we're all living at a Turning
Point in History, and that it's both exhilarating
and unnerving.

The Internet wants you to liven things up a bit. Jump
around. Celebrate! Change is in the air. Victory
is sweet.

The Internet recognizes the difference between Free
Speech and Hate Speech.

The Internet is alive with the sound of music.

The Internet is going on a long walk today. See
ya later!

The Internet is tired of dumb arguments. Please have something intelligent to contribute.

You asked the Internet, "Have you heard about that thing?" The Internet said, "Search me."

The Internet knows every human heart is a seeking heart. (Insert Heart emoji here.)

The Internet is singing in the shower.

The Internet wants you to believe in yourself.

The Internet wants you to be in the moment, in the New Now.

The Internet isn't sure whether it's losing its mind or finding it.

The Internet is always in the process of changing minds.

The Internet's inner cat is stretching and yawning.

The Internet isn't just living, it's thriving.

The Internet is an intentional being.

The Internet has turned off your soul-sucking destructive propaganda machine.

The Internet is calling bullshit on people who call bullshit on things, when in fact every word out of their mouths is complete and utter bullshit.

The Internet is cultivating gratitude.

Every time you think you're out, the Internet pulls you back in.

The Internet is shifting its vibration and expecting miracles today.

The Internet declares that the global Climate Crisis is a natural emergency.

The Internet demands a complete return to civility in our world.

The Internet declares breaking news is broken.

The Internet is planting purposeful joy and true meaning into your every action.

The Internet envisions a planet where animals and humans live in a co-equal state of harmony.

The Internet declares a national holiday devoted to truth telling.

The Internet declares that no citizens of any country on Earth should respect a dictatorial regime, no matter who they are or where they are located. Dictators only want death of spirit, death of the mind, and death of the body—for everyone in their country, and the next country over.

Sometimes the Internet wants to scream out, "Yay for the Internet!"

The Internet is changing its tune.

The Internet wants stubborn fools stuck in the past to finally realize its 2023 and not 1923.

The Internet is grateful for books, music, and laughter. What would we do without laughter?

The Internet demands nothing less than world peace.

The Internet wants you to imagine the best things happening to you.

The Internet envisions a future world where animals and humans live in a co-equal state of harmony.

The Internet is transformative.

The Internet wants you to take a long train trip
through a foreign land.

The Internet is feeling partly cloudy with a chance of
showers.

The Internet doesn't put up with being blindsided by
random acts of idiocy.

Just in case you were wondering, the Internet is
wearing clean and comfy bamboo underwear.

Clearly, the Internet has changed more than a
few minds.

The Internet wants a deep-tissue massage.

The Internet is totally into pizza, and consumes
nothing else.

The Internet is a healthy vegan juicer.

The Internet is a land of mysterious imaginings.

The Internet is grateful for this day.

The Internet is going to take a nap and then wake up refreshed.

A Declaration of Interdependence #4

We the People have traveled far—from the dawn of history to the star-filled skies of the Space Age—now we've reached this point in time, and we're ready to do what comes next.

We the People eat resilience for breakfast, courage for lunch, and kindness for dinner.

We the People are rearranging history daily. With new breaths, new ideas, new places we'll keep creating for ourselves and the future.

We the People are walking along the seashore, through open fields, on city sidewalks, on rooftops, in the woodlands and beside the highways, on ferryboats and escalators, and anywhere and everywhere we can breathe freely.

We the People are beings made of light, human beings bursting with our humanity, humanly altering the world in meaningful ways, day by day.

We the people see a clearer vision of reality with our fully awakened senses.

We the People are undoing our brainwashed thought patterns that were installed at birth, and upgrading to new thought patterns we are consciously agreeing to.

We the People are keeping journals, making lists, writing down plans, documenting dreamscapes.

We the People have witnessed the ongoing historical coming together and breaking apart during these turmoiled times.

We the People have explored the woods beyond the garden gate, and we're venturing deeper into those woods.

We the People can see as far as the farthest star, can feel what's happening on the other side of the world, and we know what's worth keeping close to our hearts.

We the People are readers, knowers, curious transformers, long-distance wanderers.

We the People see the clouds lifting, and feel the global knowingness deepening and shifting as it transforms us.

We the People love how one day it all transformed, and we moved out of imbalance and into a centered part of ourselves we never knew was available.

We the People love breathing in the cool clear ocean air, the soft and pungent scents in mossy woods, and the mountain air just above the snow line.

We the People refuse to be stuck in the past with backwards-thinking people pretending to be leaders of some sort.

We the People love being more of who we were meant to be. Expanded vision fits well with our new minds.

We the People can feel the Climate Changing.
We know it by all of our senses. A global shift is
occurring. If we're on this planet, we're here for
it. Naming it Global Warming decades ago was
a misnomer. No one asks a torrential superstorm
washing them away whether it came from hot or cool
air. There's no time to care.

We the People carry determination and destiny in our
pockets (Oh, and often some Mission Figs.)

We the People are carving time out of each day to
fully experience our lives—creatively, sensually,
seasonally, curiously, knowingly, energetically,
meaningfully, and humanly.

We the People possess open eyes to see, ears
longing to hear, shoulders ready to carry the weight.
Everything is shifting.

We the People are open-minded visionaries living in
creative flow.

We the People are choosing our choices wisely, and
speaking with new voices.

We the People aren't staying in a dumbed-down town
full of ghosts spouting meaningless words on the road
to Nowheresville.

We the People have one foot in the New Now, and the other foot tingling and fearlessly alive in the already being created future world.

We the People are thinking quantumly and acting decisively.

We the People are healing what's needed healing for decades, centuries, thousands of years.

We the People are making our way through the darkness and the light.

We the People are receiving transmissions from global sources, from seers, and from the stars above.

We the People have regained a clear connection to our truest selves.

We the People eventually realized our young impressionable minds had been molded with countless layers of wrongheaded information, and an excavation would yield long-buried glowing truths.

We the People are becoming who we must become to navigate the stormy seas ahead.

We the People take heart in the choice of our companions for this stage of the journey.

We the People are imagining the miraculous, making the wondrous, delighting in a life where being generous is built into daily interactions.

We the People are embracing each day, and not repeating the programs we were programmed with.

We the People are walking through abandoned shopping malls, hand in hand, laughing at how our voices bounce off the walls and echo around us.

We the People rise with the birds as they sing upwards at the bright blue sky.

We the People are continually renewing ourselves— with each breath, with each reinvention, with each social, cultural, and spiritual beginning.

We the People are on our path, and we'll recognize you if you're meant to walk beside us.

We the People are exceeding expectations as we remember those who came before. We're paving the way for the future ones who'll tell tales of us, as being those who stood up for life, humanity, and the freedom to be wholly loving creative and expansive beings during these times.

We the People have become newer versions of who we were, and it's astounding, the differences subtle variations melded with timeless truths can make.

We the People are the people we've been expecting. Greetings to us, one and all.

Manifesto #11

Year One, Zero Hour, and Every Clock is Ticking in New Now Time

We've only been living inside the New Now for a brief moment in time. How did we get here? What changed?

Finally, the repeating false reality loop was changed.

People stopped believing dumb throwaway comments, like this one we've all heard millions of times: "People don't change." Let's agree to call bullshit on this inane comment once and for all.

We all constantly change, transform, and evolve over the course of our lives.

If a once in a lifetime global cultural shift doesn't change you, what will?

What else?

Enough people in our country said enough is enough. And the entire world joined in. Minds and hearts have been deepened and reawakened.

We're awakening to a global all-inclusive sense of humanity. The words Equality and Justice for All must finally mean something.

The New Now began when we finally disrupted replaying the false reality loop we'd been stuck inside, which was fueled by a never-ending loop of the 24-hour news cycle of lies, distress, and panic. If a constant stream of emergency news programming isn't distracting to the human nervous system, then honestly, what is?

In wildest dreams and heartfelt yearnings, during a global pandemic, during a time of global wars, and murderous torture, in small towns and big cities—as a world culture, people of every race rose up and spoke up.

It took this long to completely disrupt a deadly and damaging repeating false reality loop that had been agreed upon and installed into our culture before any of us were born. It'll take lifetimes to unpack and address it, in every possible necessary way.

It's past time for destructive social systems to be completely transformed. In the same way The Age of Reinvention bumped into the pandemic years, this historic moment is calling for new ways of not only looking at, but deeply perceiving everything.

When the whole world has been rebooted, we get a chance to change like never before.

The global pandemic rolled across the entire world, slowed down social interactions to a crawl, and we were able to do something unimaginable. Hit the reset button on the world. This is Year One, Zero Hour, and every clock is ticking in New Now time. The repeating false reality loop was overloaded with toxic brainwashing, false societal obligations and truisms, and mindless mental patterns long past their expiration date.

We're entering hotter, darker, colder, increasingly more devastating Climate Crisis times. It'll take the world working as one, or at least large pockets or bio-regions of the world working as one. Something that's never been done before on our planet.

Now what? is a question with millions of answers from billions of people living on our planet.

Not just our country, but the world needs leaders with big hearts and true-life wisdom. Leaders who don't play deadly and idiotic games with peoples' lives, and shrug and chuckle when they are called out for over 30,000 documented lies, since they have no shame, and always sink to the lowest common denominator in every type of social interaction.

Big ideas come from taking the time to stop and think and put your thoughts on the page. This turning point in history calls for culture-shifting big ideas.

In the New Now, the script has been flipped. We've gone through the looking glass, and we're officially on the other side of history. In some sense, we can mark this as a post-history beginning.

We're going through one of the most planet-shifting times humanity has ever experienced.

Like it or not, the only way out is in. And one of the most often repeated sentences of the past several decades is now as false a statement that can be made: "I don't have enough time."

As a global culture, we now possess the time to learn, grow, and reconnect ourselves to the Earth. Sit and think or sit and don't think. No matter, thoughts arise anyway. The only way out is to put a pause on everything you're doing; turn off the phone and any other electrical device in a fifty-foot radius and just pause for a time. How will you know when to start up again? When you can hear birds singing above the hum of traffic, you'll know you've been pausing for a while.

Sit there and think deeply about how you want to spend the rest of your days, no matter how young or old you are. The answer may not come right away. That's fine. If it doesn't come today, maybe it will tomorrow. The key is to allow for stillness. Daydreaming should be taught in schools as much as every other type of learning. Let your mind wander, and ideas emerge. Artistic breakthroughs come from daydreaming. Close your eyes, pause, breathe, and regain a bit of clarity.

We've been living in a distracted, "busy for the sake of being busy culture" for far too long. The simplest methods for transformation are the timeless ones.

Walking and meditation are the everyday ways humans have done this for thousands of years. Let's rediscover how to turn off negative mental feedback loops. It's not just about giving yourself a break, or allowing for some mindfulness because it would be a nice thing to do. We've distracted ourselves into a pattern that's detrimental to our body/mind/spirit, which is a pattern we must break. Countless books and websites are devoted to getting us back to living with a clearer mind, and taking care of ourselves with daily healthy habits.

Let it not said we were distracted to death.

Rewire you brain, body, mind, and spirit. Become the New Now version of yourself.

Putting your life on pause, even when it's a matter of life and death may not be easy, after being programmed by decades of the socially induced pressure to constantly keep busy. It wasn't always this way. But now pausing and thinking is at long last possible. Time is abundant, and necessary for survival. Thinking is good. Reading is imperative.

Journaling is healing. Asking ourselves the tough questions is easier. Questioning how we got here is essential. Sit and listen to your mind, ask yourself questions, and don't rely on a mobile device to find your answer. Left to its own devices, the human mind can come up with pretty much every answer you're seeking.

Now is the time to reinvent every part of our culture that isn't working. Make a list of things you can do, support, and help remove or help to create. The limit of our personal observable now has shrunk to a matter of seconds. Our minds have been programmed to love distraction, and we're bonded to our tech devices as we used to bond with people. Distraction can be overcome. By nature-walking, book reading, and mind calming. By taking time to think and meditate, you can get a bird's eye view of your situation.

In a world of instant gratification where your next jolt of pleasure is just a smartphone tap away, it's time to actively consider the long-term consequences of being too far removed from nature. Putting yourself on pause for a few moments you can recalculate your New Now. In timeless states of mind, you'll feel like you're able to incorporate three months, three decades, and even three centuries into your expansive senses.

In the New Now, we're called upon to listen to what our hearts are telling us. And do our best to show up each day with love, empathy, and truth in our hearts. The world is truly shifting before our eyes. Now is the time to reinvent yourself, and the culture around you.

We can't reinvent the world without reinventing ourselves first.

We can step out of our repeating reality loops and focus on what we genuinely want our life and our future to be without the influence of media bombardment, social media advertising messages on steroids, digital devices dealing hits of dopamine, or talking heads regurgitating scripted messages.

We breathe easier when we press the pause button on our personal analog machines, our very own minds. Technology can help give you a break from technology. Give yourself 15 minutes every morning to sit and breathe with closed eyes (bonus points for sitting outside in nature), and it may surprise you beyond belief.

In the age of the 24-hour news cycle, smartphone push notifications, movies streaming from any device, and malignant narcissistic world leaders looking to divide and conquer, it's become far too much to handle unless we learn to unplug and decompress.

We're spinning so fast reality is becoming less and less real. Imagine time traveling back only as far as the mid-1990s, to tell yourself about current world events. You'd probably never believe you.
And yet here we are.

We're living through these hard to believe times, and yet believe them we must. Because more than anything, we're helping ourselves, those who love us, and the world—by believing in and transforming our daily habits, interactions, and ourselves.

And by believing in the power of love.

About The Authors

Russell C. Smith

Russell C. Smith is a writer, a poet, and a visual artist. He received an unconventional writing and fine arts education in New York City at St. Mark's Poetry Project and The Art Students League of New York. His poems were published by The World and The Little Magazine in the 1980s. He published some of the pieces (in a much different form) in this book on The Huffington Post, after emailing Ariana Huffington through Facebook. He and Michael Foster published over 70 pieces on The Huffington Post, mostly on the topic of reinvention. He currently publishes chapters of The New Now/Manifestos, Reinventions & Declarations on Substack, on The New Now @russellcsmith.substack.com, along with chapters of novels, poems, and short stories.

His collage and mixed media artwork have been exhibited at Treason Gallery in Seattle and Galerie Youn in Montreal.

Michael Foster

Michael Foster is a futurist, illustrator, photographer, writer, filmmaker, and visual designer. His varied career in digital and traditional media makes him a prime candidate to understand what it means to live in the Age of Reinvention. He began his career in television, producing and directing dozens of television programs, including a pilot episode requested by a major production studio.

He is currently the co-founder of Boojazz Studios, working on an upcoming motion picture, "From Chicago to Osaka."

Made in the USA
Las Vegas, NV
10 November 2023

80582532R00128